The Transport of Hope

How one humanitarian made a difference in the Balkan conflict

The Transport of Hope

How one humanitarian
made a difference in the Balkan conflict

Jeanne McCue
Peg Masterson Edquist

Milwaukee, Wisconsin

Photographs by the author or used with permission.

Published by
HenschelHAUS Publishing, Inc.
www.henschelHAUSbooks.com

ISBN: 978-1-59598-446-3
E-ISBN: 978-1-59598-447-0
AUDIO ISBN: 978-1-59598-448-7
LCCN: 2015959426

Printed in the United States of America.

A portion of the proceeds from the sale of this book go to support refugee assistance.

To my son Daniel

Table of Contents

Foreword i
Acknowledgments v

Preface 1

Chapter 1: Journey into Darkness 5
Chapter 2: Finding My Way in the Dark 13
Chapter 3: Evil Hates Bridges 27
Chapter 4: The Early Years of Hope 51
Chapter 5: Sarajevo: The Saddest Town in the World 69
Chapter 6: The Roots of Home Sprout a Forest 95
Chapter 7: The Narrow Road 107

Resources and References 123
About the Authors 125

Foreword

Heroes come in all sizes, pixies as well as giants. One of my favorite people in the world could be overlooked in an empty room. But she has never limited her determination. Her bravery couldn't be measured with a ruler. Her heart is about the same size as ours, until she puts it to use.

Jeanne McCue is a primary example of the power of one. For years, Jeanne, a nurse, collected medical supplies in her home; went to doctors, nurses, administrators, hospitals, clinics, and begged supplies for people battered by war; filled her basement, stuffed her closets, built mountains of syringes and bandages and cotton balls in her garage. Once or twice a year, she paid her own way to fly to the Balkans, where she distributed the supplies to people whose lives had been brutalized by a senseless war among Croatians, Serbs and Muslims. She didn't care who the enemy was, only the hurt.

Motivated by her faith, and her knowledge that deprived people desperately needed the supplies, she flew to them, as if she had wings. Besides bringing tons of supplies, she brought her hugs and her hope.

During the early 1990s, I was with her in Medjugorje, when the war was only a few miles away. Men fought on the front lines for days, then hitch-hiked, took taxis, or hopped a bus for home. For a few days, they ate hot meals, took showers, hugged their wives and kids. Then they called for taxis, and headed back to the front. Their ambulance was a station wagon. They bought their own bullets.

Jeanne and I drove into Mostar, a town the war had devastated; our driver told us to crouch down as we crossed certain streets, which snipers used as straight-aways for their weapons. We stopped at an old hospital, with a new hospital being built next door. Shelling had put holes in the upper floors of the new building so the old place was still used, where some corridors were jammed with the beds of patients. In the basement, sick children were nursed, windows rattled, walls shaking with the sounds of large weapons continuing the war outside.

The children didn't seem to notice, they were too busy noticing Jeanne. She had brought them dolls and all the love she had. She knew that for kids, stuffed animals were often the medicine the kids needed, as the windows shook.

She brought her precious supplies, which she'd collected on nights and weekends and days off, when she wasn't working her regular job. But she hadn't forgotten what those children in Mostar needed most: her hugs and a little stuffed elephant with pink eyes.

In those days, while much of the rest of the world turned their backs on the dead and dying in Bosnia, volunteers, such as Jeanne, refused to take that dreadful position of non-involvement. She drove through the night on icy mountain roads to get her first supplies to Sarajevo, when cargo planes didn't land regularly. After one of her first trips there, a bullet hole was found in one of the iced windows in the vehicle she had been in.

Foreword

I saw her bring hope to families living in boxcars, still on railroad tracks that war had blocked. She asked permission to hold the sick, and hug the hurt. I've insisted that Jeanne McCue is a saint, without the consecration.

What she accomplished, she accomplished by thinking of people who needed her, and nothing stopped her from going to them. She'd had her own tragedies, but concentrated on the tragedies of others.

One bitterly cold winter night, she came home to her empty home in a Milwaukee suburb. She was lonely, I'm sure. She was probably tired, but tiredness is perpetual with nurses. It's as common as the will to help. In her home that night, she noticed one of her late son's warm winter coats; she took her son's coat, brought it to her car, and drove to downtown Milwaukee in the middle of the night. She cruised the dark streets until she saw a homeless man, shivering in the cold. She stopped the car, gave him the coat, got back into the car, and drove home.

I've told myself that a standing ovation would certainly be appropriate for the way Jeanne McCue has lived her life, but, at my age, I don't know if I could endure what I'd need to do. I'd be standing all the time.

—Bill Janz

Milwaukee Sentinel columnist

Acknowledgments

I will always be grateful to my niece and co-author, Peg Masterson Edquist, who for the last 24 years has been a part of my missions. She has encouraged me to tell my stories, which she has so skillfully transformed to show the joy of giving when serving others. Through the years, she has collected, packed, and transported supplies, prayed, and traveled with me to Sarajevo, Bosnia. Thank you, Peg, for your patience and determination to make *Transport of Hope* possible.

I wish to thank my friends who accompanied me on many of my 40 missions, especially Pat Roell and Irene Haliday, who made multiple trips. I am grateful for generous donors for their faithful support and prayers during the years and my Croatian friends in Milwaukee for their friendship, support and sharing their ethnic traditions.

Thanks to all my "Muffin" friends in Whitefish Bay who sorted, packed, labeled, and lifted hundreds of boxes of humanitarian aid all hours of the day and evening.

I am grateful to my family and daughter Kerry for her support and to my grandchildren, who inspire me as they now serve others.

I thank Brother Thomas O'Grady, whom I met through a meaningful coincidence in the Split, Croatia, airport and who made it possible for me to enter Sarajevo in 1995 to transport and distribute humanitarian aid to people in desperate need and for his friendship through the years.

I am grateful to all my drivers and interpreters through the years and to the dear Franciscan Sisters at Provare Street in Sarajevo who provided a safe haven and warm hospitality whenever I visit.

Nothing is impossible with God at our side. I praise and thank God for leading me to Bosnia and for His many blessings that helped me bring help and hope to a desperate people in a war-torn country.

Preface

1990 seemed to be a year of hopefulness. Lech Walesa became president of Poland, Nelson Mandela was released from prison, and the demolition of the Berlin Wall officially began. It was a time of optimism as the end of the Cold War brought the promise of peace and possibility.

But one year later, in 1991, a horrific war in Yugoslavia was in its genesis. It was also the year I first visited that country, and my life would never be the same.

When the Soviet Union broke up in 1991, Eastern Europe was thrown into chaos. This was never more apparent than in the Socialist Federal Republic of Yugoslavia. It was a country made up of six socialist republics—Bosnia-Herzegovina, Croatia, Macedonia, Montenegro, Serbia, and Slovenia—all of which strove for more autonomy. The region rapidly spiraled into war and out of the conflict came the leader of Serbia, Slobodan Milosevic. He was the most cunning of all the rulers and also the most dangerous.

The ensuing war and genocide saw a civilian population besieged by bombing, sniper attacks, mass shootings and assaults against women throughout the country. It was impossible for me to look away once I had visited that place just a year earlier on a pilgrimage to Medjugorje, an internationally renowned religious site in Bosnia-Herzegovina.

The Transport of Hope

When my son died unexpectedly at age 27, I was encouraged to travel to Medjugorje, where fellow Catholics were going on pilgrimages because of visions children had reportedly seen of the Blessed Virgin. I went on the trip somewhat reluctantly, but once I landed, I felt comforted and renewed. I also fell in love with the country and the Serbs, Croats, and Muslims who lived in that beautiful part of the world.

When war broke out the next year, I knew I had to return to help the wounded, the refugees, and the children. That was more than 24 years and 40 trips ago. Along the way, I've been able to bring medical supplies, medicine, hygiene packs, knitting needles, goats, shoes, toys, money—and lots and lots of hope.

The people who became my donors have my utmost gratitude. I was never without support from friends, family, and many strangers who were drawn to my efforts and gave whatever they could.

I have found that people who really want to make a difference go largely unnoticed as they do their work. With fierce determination, they are sustained and encouraged by a smile from an elderly person or the hug from a orphaned child. These are all they need to carry on. That is why I have made these trips again and again. And I am not alone. I am part of an unorganized army of private citizens who bring necessary aid into areas of hatred, pain, and suffering.

Even though the war in Bosnia-Herzegovina officially ended with the Dayton Peace Accord in 1995, the need for support continues. Lives were shattered, the orphan population became a generation of young adults with no families, and unemployment and poverty have become a way of life. The people I have met along the way are a part of my life forever. From the diabetic children in Zavidovici to a wonderful family who lived through the siege in Sarajevo, to an Irish brother who assisted with my missions, and to the sisters on Provare Street in Sarajevo who hosted me for twenty years. They are all family to me.

When I look at our current world that is once again dominated by hatred and violence, I feel the need to make known the importance of the message of peace, hope, and joy. I've learned that small changes can make a big difference. We all need to continue to work for peace, to live with hope and joy in our hearts, and bring that hope to people who have lost it. Many of them are our neighbors who need to see that the human race must stand together and promote acceptance and peace.

I hope my story will encourage others to realize that they can make a difference in the world, regardless of their circumstances. To bring incremental improvement, no matter how small, is a act of true selflessness, and in return, it can bring happiness, contentment, and a feeling of fulfillment.

I would not have missed it for the world!

—Jeanne McCue

CROATIA
Sava R.
Una R.
Prijedor
Kozarac
Omarska
Bihać
Sana R.
Vrbas R.
Banja Luka
Bosna R.
Brčko
Bijeljina
Drina R.
Tuzla
Zvornik
SERBIA
Una R.
Jajce
Travnik
Vitez
Zenica
Srebrenica
BOSNIA
Bosna R.
Kupres
Sarajevo
Žepa
Pale
Rogatica
Tomislavgrad
Goražde
Višegrad
CROATIA
Neretva R.
Drina R.
Split
Foča
Mostar
Medjugorje
MONTENEGRO
Adriatic Sea
Trebinje
0 Miles 30
0 Kilometers 50
Dubrovnik
GERMANY
CZECH REP.
UKRAINE
FRANCE
Danube R.
SLOVAKIA
MOLDOVA
AUSTRIA
SWITZ.
HUNGARY
ROMANIA
SLOVENIA
Zagreb
Sava R.
CROATIA
BOSNIA
Belgrade
SERBIA
Danube R.
ITALY
Adriatic Sea
Priština
BULGARIA
MONTENEGRO
MACEDONIA
ALBANIA
0 Miles 200
0 Kilometers 320
GREECE
TURKEY

Chapter 1
Journey into Darkness

The sound of mortar shells landing and exploding is terrifying. The shells are on their way to obliterate a target, and that might be you. When the attack has passed, left behind is a surreal scene of buildings spewing smoke, smoldering and in ruins. Is this a nightmare? Later in the day, the sound of sniper fire comes from the hills above. Leaving your apartment to get food and water is tempting fate. The pungent odor of fire and gas and death is all around.

In 1992, the people of Bosnia Herzegovina were enveloped in terror that would not end. Hate had entered the city of Sarajevo and would not leave. In this place, there was no love or family, no faith or kindness, no humanity or civilization.

Sometimes the hand of God takes you to places you never imagined. My many journeys to Bosnia and the world of war, destruction, and obliteration were by choice. From my quiet existence in Whitefish Bay, a suburb of Milwaukee, I traveled for more than two decades to a place no one wanted to go, but where I had to go to deal with my grief through helping others.

In 1989, my son Daniel was found dead on a bike path in northern Wisconsin. He was 27 years old. As a mother, I was inextricably linked to my child. I felt his pain, his joy and his sadness without any words being spoken. As I found out more about Daniel's remarkable life, I felt drawn to do something to carry on his memory.

Daniel was a sensitive, generous, caring, and thoughtful young man. He was only 10 when his father died. He was interested in biking, electronics, having friends over to watch *Laurel & Hardy* movies, and doing kind deeds for others. He was a Boy Scout and a paper boy. He also battled depression. It was only days after his death that I started to hear of his quiet generosity to others.

To give without notice
has a special quality of its own.
—Anne Morrow Lindbergh

Many years ago, our parish priest, Father Bob Wells, spoke in his homily of a young man who passed some children who were selling their art work for 50 cents on a lawn near the church. The young man gave each of the children $5 for their art. The children later told our priest how excited they were. They ran to tell their mother about the generous man who gave them more than they had asked. After mass, I complimented Father Bob on a great homily. He told me that the young man was his friend and my son, Daniel.

More than 20 years later, when I am feeling low, I go into Daniel's bedroom to look at those works of art. They remind me of who he was and how he inspired me to change my life in ways that I could never have dreamed of.

After Daniel died, I learned that he had sent donations to CARE and Doctors Without Borders. How had he realized that giving and kindness were the best parts of being human? How had I not been able to see all of these wonderful attributes? It was almost as if Danny had mapped out my future. His life had been headed in a direction that I needed to go. I had to find a way to keep his generosity alive. At that point, I didn't realize I was soon to be headed on a path to do just that.

As I left my home on my 40th mission to Bosnia-Herzegovina in September 2015, I recalled the first trip of hope I made in June 1992. I was about to go to a new and unknown destination—a country at war. Since then, that beautiful country with its rich history has become my second home, always welcoming and calling me back. I have grown to love its customs, its food, and so many friends who are now like family. How could I ever say good-bye?

It is not too uncommon for people to look for something to explain, comfort, or distract them after a tragic event in their life. A year after Danny's death, a friend of mine encouraged me to take a pilgrimage to Medjugorje, a little village in the mountains of Bosnia-Herzegovina (formerly known as Yugoslavia). At that time, the country was run by the Tito Communist government. I could never know then that my first pilgrimage would open the door to a whole new world—a world of challenge, commitment, caring and more priceless experiences than I could ever dream of.

The meaning of pilgrimage —a journey not only to a place like Medjugorje, but the journey which comes after and lasts the rest of one's life.
—Father Svetozar Kraljevic, OFM

The Transport of Hope

My first pilgrimage to Medjugorje was in 1990, a year before the Balkan war. How could I have known my life would be forever changed? I have always marveled at the wisdom of God. He knows what we need and when we need it!

A priest in my parish was taking a group to Medjugorje, and a good friend who had been there persuaded me to join the group. Since 1981, in that small mountain village, the Blessed Virgin Mary was making daily apparitions to six young children, bringing messages of hope, peace, and forgiveness. Tens of thousands of pilgrims from all over the world still travel to Medjugorje to pray at St. James Church and witness the place where the Holy mother gave the world those messages.

Even though I told my friend that I did not like to travel, I agreed to go. A few days before departure, I was diagnosed with phlebitis in my leg and was at risk of developing a clot during the long transatlantic flight. I decided to take my chances, elevating and moving my leg during the flight. The pain and swelling left as soon as I arrived in Medjugorje.

Our group flew JAG, Yugoslav Airlines, to Mostar, a city 50 kilometers from Medjugorje. The airport was drab and colorless, filled with armed Yugoslav Army guards. We boarded a bus and drove across the rugged Herzegovina mountains. The mountains, I would learn, were a central feature in the lives of the Croatians.

The general population did not make much of a living, but they needed little. They were satisfied with what they had. The Croatians seemed to take on the character of the mountains. They were calm, steady, quiet, and enduring. I was struck by the simplicity of the people and their strong faith.

As we entered the village, I could see the twin spires of St. James Church. It had been rebuilt in 1969 to accommodate thousands of worshipers, even though the village had only 400 families at the time.

In those days, Catholic villagers and Franciscan priests lived in fear of the government. They were still suffering under Tito's regime. Under Communism in Bosnia-Herzegovina and Croatia, people were not promoted according to the quality of their work, discipline, or honesty, but by their loyalty to the Communist Party and obedience to their supervisors.

The Catholic church posed a threat to Communism. In Herzegovina, priests were murdered. Others were thrown in prisons for months and years, where they faced solitary confinement and torture. In times of great adversity, the church thrives and the faith of its people becomes stronger.

Initially, the government harassed pilgrims flocking to Medjugorje. Army helicopters would hover over the church and guesthouses to remind people of their presence in the area.

The parish priest, Fr. Jozo Zovka, was arrested and sentenced to three and a half years in prison. Thanks to protests on his behalf, he was released after 18 months.

By 1983, the state realized that nothing in its power could stop the influx of pilgrims from abroad and recognized the considerable financial contribution to the local economy.

As a fellow pilgrim, I was struck by this mystical place, where faith was in full view. This journey was not about my life, but about how the trials and challenges of our lives become lighter when we help others carry their burdens. One of my personal beliefs that gives me strength comes from St. Matthew:

Come to me, all who are weary and find life burdensome. I will refresh you. Take my yoke upon your shoulders and learn from me, for I am gentle and humble of heart. Your soul will find rest, for my burden is light.
—Matthew 11:28-30

The year after my pilgrimage, the Balkan war broke out. I was heartbroken that the kind and generous people in the villages I had come to know were in the midst of a terrible military conflict. On television at home, I watched in horror as suffering and death were portrayed. Those images touched my heart. I would never be the same and I immediately knew my calling—to help those wonderful people in whatever way I could.

Ever since I was a young girl, I wanted to be a nurse. Nursing is a calling, a way of giving oneself to enhance the lives of others, to make a difference. As a young nursing student, I loved to read about Florence Nightingale. In 1820, she served on the front lines of the Crimean War and improved hospital conditions to help soldiers who suffered from their wounds, as well as from typhus and cholera.

In nursing school in the 1950s, I worked with the Daughters of Charity of St. Vincent de Paul. They allowed me to accompany them on their visits to the poor in Milwaukee's inner city, where I would help distribute food and clothing. Through those early experiences, I learned the joy of giving.

One of my dreams was to help others in far-away lands, even in a war zone. After the war in Bosnia began, I reached out to an organization in the United States that was delivering medicine and other supplies. As a registered nurse, I was qualified to accompany the plane. The memories from that first trip and the reality of experiencing war first hand touched my heart deeply—the vast destruction of homes and property, and the pain and suffering of innocent people.

When I returned home after one week, the images of the people in need gave me the desire to go back to Bosnia again and again. It has been gratifying to bring aid directly to anyone involved in the war, not just people of one religion or ethnic group, but everyone who was hungry, sick and injured. We are all God's people.

Bringing humanitarian aid became my calling. I would go on to start a grassroots humanitarian organization. I wanted to show those affected by war that they were not alone or forgotten. The West did not intervene until the massacres in the marketplaces in Sarajevo at Srebrenica.

The stories of the hardships and a growing population of refugees called to me to bring aid. I was on my way to where it was needed most.

Jeanne McCue with a refugee child in Mostar (1993)

Jeanne McCue distributing aid to children in Medjugorje (1993)

Chapter 2
Finding My Way in the Dark

In 1984, after the winter Olympics in Sarajevo, Yugoslavia was a place of peace. It was made up of six different yet united republics: Croatia, Serbia, Montenegro, Macedonia, Bosnia-Herzegovina, and Slovenia. The country's leader, wartime resistance hero Josip Broz Tito, had governed the country from 1945 until his death in 1980. Under his rule, being Yugoslav mattered more than Muslim or Christian, Croat or Serb.

Sarajevo embodied the historic waves of culture, religions, and traditions that had swept across the country over the centuries. In several of the neighborhoods, small wooden-fronted shops and cobblestone streets resembled a quaint village from another time. In her book, *The Key to My Neighbor's House*, author Elizabeth Neuffer recalled the smell of spicy kebab wafting through the air, recalling the days of the Ottoman Empire.

This ancient city had mosques, Orthodox churches and Catholic cathedrals. It was a blend of Europe and the Orient, a city with a multiethnic population; many intermarried. Even today, when I visit the city long after the devastation of the war, the smells, tastes and sounds of Sarajevo move me deeply.

In 1989, things began to change. A rising nationalist politician named Slobodan Milosevic from Serbia held a rally in the Serbian province of Kosovo. The rally was held to commemorate the 600th anniversary of the Battle of Kosovo in 1389, when Serb forces tried to defend against the Ottoman Turks and lost. In June 1989, nearly one million Serbs went to Kosovo and cheered wildly for Milosevic. Things were never the same.

Communism was collapsing across Eastern Europe, and nationalism was taking its place, spawning new leaders hungry for power. In Yugoslavia, the stirrings of political change came in the wake of Tito's death and the nationalistic crisis he left behind.

Once hailed at the richest and most open of the Communist economies, Yugoslavia was on the verge of financial collapse, with some $20 billion in foreign debt. Economic hard times had arrived in most of Europe in the 1980s. Europe began cutting back on jobs for the Yugoslavs, who worked in neighboring countries, and unemployment soared. Inflation surged, hitting 250 percent in 1989. Industries floundered, workers went on strike, and political chaos reigned. The collective presidency formed after Tito's death didn't work, allowing power to devolve back to the republics, many of which were dominated by one ethnicity.

The situation played into the hands of Milosevic, a ruthless Serb politician. His father, mother, and uncle had committed suicide while he was growing up. He went on to study law at Belgrade University and became a banker, spending time in New York. He returned to Yugoslavia and married Mirjana Markovic. Tremendously ambitious, he climbed his way up the political ranks and ended up as head of the Serbian Communist Party.

A speech in 1987 in Kosovo extolled Milosevic's support of Kosovo Serbs over the ethnic Albanian majority. He portrayed Serbs as a heroic and glorious people who had suffered centuries of injustice because of frustrated efforts to have their own state. Now was the time of reckoning: Serbs needed to have their own nation.

Milosevic's call for a greater Serbia would destroy Yugoslavia. Soon Croatia and Serbia were at war, driven by nationalist and ethnic discontent. Milosevic imported the war to Bosnia, which had lived peacefully as a multi-ethnic country since the early Middle Ages.

Milosevic fanned the flames of nationalist hatred until Bosnia erupted into an ethnic inferno. Neighbor turned on neighbor, Christian against Muslim, Serb against Croat. The result was a collective madness that spawned mass executions, torture, rape, the expulsion of millions of civilians from their homes, and the rebirth of concentration camps.

Within a few years of Tito's death, everything that happened to the people depended on their ethnicity. Nationalism began to sweep across Yugoslavia in earnest.

Several months later, war broke out in the Balkans. At home in America, I saw daily television Images of suffering, death, and refugees fleeing their homes.

In the early years of the war, the West dismissed the Balkan conflict as "someone else's war." In fact, I felt that the West—Europe and America in particular—were unwilling to commit. They did not understand the Balkan war and did not want to get involved, so the war and horrors of war continued.

The Transport of Hope

In her book entitled *Survival Guide for Sarajevo,* FAMA International founder and director, Suada Kapic, describes the day the war took hold on April 5th, 1992, in that city:

> *In the very center of what was Yugoslavia, two hundred and sixty tanks appeared, one hundred and twenty mortars, and innumerable anti-aircraft cannons, sniper rifles and other small arms entered the city. They were entrenched around the city, facing it. At any moment, from any of these spots, any of these arms can hit a target in the city. And they did hit, indeed—civilian housing, museums, churches, mosques, hospitals, cemeteries, people on the streets. Everything became a target. All exits from the city, all points of entry, were blocked.*

In January 1993, broadcast journalist Martin Bell delivered an emotional and powerful report on the ABC news program *Nightline.* Bell cut through the complexities of the conflict and revealed the devastation and destruction of the war. He also acknowledged that Western intervention had not yet come and hundreds of innocent people were homeless, and were persecuted, raped, tortured and killed.

Bell said in his report, "The case for intervention is not to help one side or the other, but the weak against the strong, the unarmed against the armed."

I will never forget that newscast. At that time, I was already traveling to the country to help the refugees. Many times, I was confronted by Bosnians asking when my country would come to help.

In news reports, the world was told of the Bosnian conflict in graphic detail with thousands of images. Reports surfaced about the marketplace massacre in February 1994. That month, a high-powered shell fired by Bosnian Serb forces from the surrounding hills exploded in an outdoor marketplace in Sarajevo. The explosion killed 69 people and wounded more than 200. Bodies were strewn on the ground. Cries of help could be heard as the maimed and injured lay bleeding on the snow.

Sarajevo's people lived under the constant threat of being killed or wounded. In a split second, a shell might explode on a street or a playground, or a rocket-fired bomb would blast a hole in through an apartment-building wall. Snipers wandered the bomb-scarred neighborhoods, taking aim at anyone in their sights.

A great international outcry went up after the massacre. NATO demanded that the Serbs pull back their weapons. After a brief respite from the violence, terror struck the city when an outdoor shopping area in Sarajevo was attacked in August 1995. The explosions killed 38 people and dozens were wounded.

During this time, reports of concentration camps, torture, and rape occurred regularly. Hospitals struggled to save lives without medicines or equipment. Stories flooded the media of children being massacred while sledding or attending improvised schools—schools without heat and electricity.

The plight of citizens struggling to exist under such conditions overwhelmed me. News reports shocked television viewers and newspaper readers around the world.

In his 1995 book, *Cry Bosnia*, author Paul Harris was convinced the West would not come to the rescue of Bosnia. "So many stories, so much blood, so much tragedy unfolded, layer upon layer, before the reader and the viewer."

Although American forces eventually came to help, years earlier, the images of the suffering moved the American public. Some of the most effective and ambitious aid efforts for Bosnia did not come from large government agencies, but from small charities, private individuals and organizations operating outside governmental channels. They cut through red tape and brought aid directly to the people.

My story is just one of many accounts of people in America who brought hope and care back into that besieged country. Like so many others, I wanted to be a part of bringing aid to these desperate people.

My First Trip of Hope

In 1992, a pilgrimage organization in Alabama needed a nurse to accompany a cargo plane full of medical supplies, food, and medicines to the Croatian and Medjugorje region. I called and requested to go, and was told to send my resume. Eagerly, I awaited a response.

The next day I was on my work at Milwaukee County Hospital. I prayed and told God that I would follow Him wherever He would lead. A few hours afterward, I received a call of acceptance and a message that I was to fly to Alabama by Sunday evening. God never wastes time.

The realization that I would be going into a war zone struck me, yet fear was not a factor. The decision was made and that night, I fell sound asleep and awoke with a tremendous feeling of peace—a deep sense of calm, quiet confidence, and trust in God.

When the war in Bosnia broke out, it was hard to realize that the holy sites of pilgrimage I had visited just a few years before were now military conflict zones. Ancient hatreds were being revived. I had to go back and help the people. As a young nursing student, I had always dreamed of helping others in a far-off land. Now I would be going into a war zone to aid the injured and minister to the helpless.

For the next few days in the heat of an Alabama June, we loaded tons of supplies by hand into a DC-8 cargo plane. Despite the heavy lifting all day, I never had an ache or a pain.

Seven of us were on that flight in cramped seats behind the food and medical supplies. It was only my second trans-Atlantic flight and a far cry from a commercial economy class flight. There were no windows on the sides of plane to offer views of our journey. Fatigued from the packing, we slept soundly on the floor of the plane until we landed to refuel in Bangor, Maine. The flight continued on to Brussels, Belgium, and 15 hours later, we arrived at Ancona, Italy.

Because Croatia was at war, airlines could not obtain insurance. Passengers and cargo were flown into Italy, then loaded onto ferries, which crossed the Adriatic to the port of Split, Croatia.

In Italy, we unpacked tons of supplies by hand and loaded boxes onto five large trucks. We traveled with the cargo to an Italian monastery, where we spent the night. The monastery housed about 30 nuns and one priest. It was on a steep hill overlooking the turquoise-blue Adriatic Sea, a beautiful and peaceful setting.

At dusk the next evening, the trucks were driven to the ferry docks and loaded onto a Croatian ferry, the *Bartol Kasic,* which had been donated for the specific purpose of transporting relief supplies to Croatia.

At the port, we met up with six men from London, England, who were donating six ambulances filled with medical supplies. I would later travel with them to deliver supplies to hospitals and village clinics in Mostar, Chitluk, and surrounding areas.

Jeanne McCue with a refugee boy, interpreter, and two humanitarian aid workers disembarking from the *Bartol Kasic* (1993)

At midnight, we boarded the ferry and in the early morning hours, arrived on the coast of Croatia at Split. We were met by a Franciscan priest, Father Svetozar Kraljevic, "Father Svet," and Gojko, an innkeeper from Medjugorje.

Gojko proved to be a reliable friend and the man whom I would later contact to help me bring my own supplies time and again to Bosnia-Herzegovina. He also knew what supplies were most needed. This invaluable information helped tremendously with later missions.

Father Svet arranged for us to drop off supplies in Herzegovina, Posusje, Grude and Mostar. We drove to Mostar, which had been bombed two days before. Many of the buildings we passed were still smoldering. For the first time, I was witnessing the effects of war, the shelling and destruction of mortars from the peaks of the mountains that overlook Mostar.

At a hospital, an ambulance arrived with children who had been injured by a booby trap while picking up objects in the street. A mother wept in the bombed-out St. Peter and Paul Church after seeing the rubble remaining where her children had been baptized and made their first Holy Communion. She stood near the only statue that had been spared—the Blessed Virgin. Fear and sadness in her eyes, as in the eyes of everyone we met that day. But I also saw hope when the people discovered we were from the United States to bring help.

We spent a week delivering supplies to clinics, hospitals and refugee camps. We visited many physicians from small villages. All were grateful for the supplies. Many of the hospitals had been bombed. Temporary hospitals were

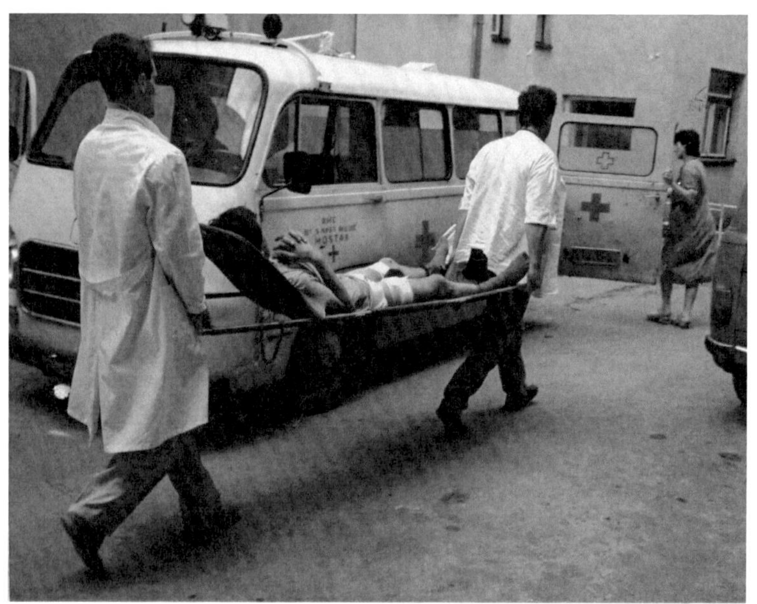

Doctors bringing the wounded to a hospital in Mostar

English ambulance drivers donate ambulances
and distribute supplies in Mostar

been set up in homes, gyms, and factories. Most of the buildings, churches, hospitals, and homes were still smoldering. The air was heavy with smoke.

The ambulances I had traveled in were put to good use just minutes after delivery to pick up the wounded and dead. Parks were turned into graveyards and filled up quickly.

I met a nine-year-old boy, Sonel, who had been placed with other children for safety on an island off the Croatian coast. He had managed to get to the mainland to look for his parents. A reporter from the *Philadelphia Inquirer* decided to follow him to Mostar, where we tried to help him find his father, who was a soldier, and his mother, who was pregnant.

Jeanne McCue unloads boxes of supplies from an ambulance in Medjugorje

A mother weeps amidst the bombed-out ruins of St. Peter & Paul Church in Mostar, where her children had been baptized and taken their first Holy Communion.

Many children like Sonel had been separated from their parents and would never find their loved ones. Thousands of refugees, desperate people driven from their homes, would never return.

Decades later, I can still see the abandoned homes and apartments, a chilling reminder of the lingering effects of war.

In the early days of the war, bread lines with food and water were set up at various corners of the city, but few people ventured out for fear of shelling or sniper fire. Many convoys of supplies were attacked. A news article reported about a Red Cross convoy bringing medicine into Sarajevo that came under fire, killing one person and injuring four others. A truck carrying 4½ tons of medicine was destroyed by a rocket.

That first week, I witnessed something much greater than suffering. The people of Bosnia-Herzegovina were full of faith and unselfishness, willing to share what little they had. Physicians who were given supplies shared with doctors in areas of greater need. The seven of us were provided lodging in convents, homes and monasteries by people who cared for us with love and kindness.

On the way home after my first mission, I felt exhausted, but elated. I had met so many wonderful people, aid workers helping those in need. I had also met destitute people who had lost everything and were living a life of deprivation. Yet the two groups had so much in common: faith, love, courage, and thankfulness in the midst of despair. I knew I wanted to be a part of it. I felt right at home. Humanitarian work is addictive!

Fresh graves in a park in Mostar (1993)

Refugee children receive toys from Jeanne McCue in Mostar (1993)

How strange it was to return home to the safety and sanity of America. Shopping at my local grocery store, where vegetables, meat, canned goods, and much more were in abundant supply, left me feeling sad and disconnected. The images of people in need had given me the impetus and desire to return to Bosnia as often as I could.

The gratitude of a refugee mother receiving food and the smiles and hugs of refugee children who had so little filled me with joy. I was grateful to be able to provide physicians with the supplies they needed to heal and ease pain.

Soon after coming back to Wisconsin, I started the Bosnia Relief Charitable Trust, whose mission was to show those affected by war that they are not alone or forgotten.

Chapter 3
Evil Hates Bridges

One of the most poignant but disturbing memories of my early trips to Bosnia-Herzegovina was the destruction of so much of the beautiful architecture. Historical buildings, stunning ancient churches, and entire towns were all but destroyed by constant shelling. Nothing made this clearer than the number of bridges that were blasted into rubble.

At one time, Mostar was the architectural and cultural jewel of Bosnia-Herzegovina. It was divided by the Neretva River, which also separated the Croatians living on the west side of the river and Muslims on the east. Five bridges connected people in the city, the most beautiful being the arched *Stari Most,* or "Old Bridge."

Stari Most was more than 450 years old and considered one of the most breathtaking bridges in the world. Built during the Ottoman Empire, the bridge was constructed under the rule of Suliman the Magnificent. He ordered a spectacular bridge to be built over the Neretva River; it was completed in 1556. The bridge survived centuries of conflict, including World War I and World War II, with only minor damage.

In 1993, the bridge succumbed to shelling. Other Mostar bridges that were demolished included the Carinski, Titov, and Lucki.

Father Svet looking over one of seven bridges bombed in Mostar

One of my key contacts during those early visits was Father Svetozar Kraljevic, a Franciscan priest who lived in Mostar, a few miles from Medjugorje. He had witnessed many atrocities and attacks on villagers, churches, and hospitals.

Father Svet took me to the highest point of a 500-year-old stone Turkish bridge that had been almost completely destroyed by bombing. This bridge had stood for centuries and served as a symbol of Mostar's multi-ethnic traditions. It was one of seven bridges that connected East Mostar (Serbs) to West Mostar (Bosnian Croats). After days of constant shelling, this bridge, like the others, had crumbled into the Neretva. As we stood there, Father Svet said to me,

"Evil hates bridges—because bridges connect and unify people. "

I first met Father Svet when he greeted us in Split, Croatia, as we were getting off the ferry from Ancona, Italy, on my first mission trip. He would accompany us through the mountains to Medjugorje.

Medjugorje was a spiritual lifeline for pilgrims and villagers alike, and a material lifeline of supplies brought in from Italy and Europe. Although war raged only a few miles away in Mostar, pilgrims still came to Medjugorje. It had not been bombed or rocketed, possibly because of the international pilgrims there, or possibly because of the United Nations tanks stationed at the edge of town.

Despite the proximity of the military conflict, the faithful filled the pews, stood in the aisles, and sat on the floor each night to attend mass at St. James Church.

Many invaluable treasures were lost between 1992 and 1993. After Bosnia declared independence from Yugoslavia, Mostar was subjected to 18 months of siege. The Yugoslavian People's Army, JNA, first bombed Mostar in April 1992. Over the following weeks, they gradually established control over a large part of the city.

By June of that year, the Croatian Defense Council Army forced the JNA out of Mostar. The JNA responded with constant shelling from the mountains above.

Throughout those months, a sustained campaign of ethnic cleansing took place. This typically entailed intimidation, mass rapes, forced expulsion, and murder of ethnic groups. Churches, cemeteries, and places of cultural and historical significance were destroyed.

Among the monuments and historic buildings destroyed in Mostar were the Franciscan Monastery, Muslim mosques, St. Peter and Paul Church, the Catholic cathedral and the Bishop's Palace, which once held more than 50,000 books.

Father Svet took me through the charred ruins of the Bishop's Palace. He told me the destruction was part of a campaign to destroy all records of births, baptisms, and deaths. As we picked our way carefully through the remains, surrounded by the pungent odor of burning and throat-clogging soot, Father Svet randomly picked up a charred Bible and scraps of pages from the Old Testament.

Those few sheets were from the Book of Daniel—the name of my deceased son. Daniel was a prophet, and there is a philosophy of history found in Daniel's visions. I have always felt that God was leading, directing, and planning my life. Picking up those scorched pages was like getting a letter from home.

When Father Svet and I walked through the burned and still smoldering ruins of St. Peter and Paul Church in Mostar, it was hardly recognizable. The roof was gone. All that remained were charred walls of what had once been a beautiful church. The gold chalice on the altar had melted, yet a statue of the Blessed Virgin stood untouched.

Father Svet's words of "evil hating bridges" reminded me that evil truly does hate bridges—but not only bridges made of brick and mortar. Bridges of friendship and communication allow people to help one another, which ultimately leads to peace.

During my personal journey, I have had the privilege of being a bridge between the people of Bosnia and the people

...ICNE P...

»*Blago onima, koji prebivaju u domu* ...
de, hvaliće Te na vijeke vjekova.« Ovako se (po ps. 83) čita
na Pričesti današnje sv. Mise.

Predragi! Želite li i vi osjetiti sreću prebivanja u domu Gospodnjemu, u nebu? Treba da se riješite grijeha. »*Jer ovo znajte i zapamtite* — govori sv. Pavao u današnjoj Epistoli — *da nijedan bludnik ili nečist ili lakomac* (ili sa bilo kojim smrtnim grijehom na duši) *nema dijela u kraljevstvu Isukrstovu i Božjem.*«

Ovo sveto korizmeno doba nadasve je zgodno da ustanemo od grijeha. Zato je sv. Crkva i naredila u ovo doba *sv. Ispovijed* i uskrsnu Pričest. Ta je naredba velika i veoma važna, veže pod smrtni grijeh.

Ima među vjernicima, Bogu hvala, koji ne čekaju Korizmu, nego se i više puta u godini isipovijede i pričeste. Ali ih, nažalost ima, ne mali broj koji tolike i tolike godine zanemare godišnju Ispovijed i uskrsnu Pričest. To su kao onaj nijemi u današnjem sv. Evanđelju, koga je đavao držao u svojoj vlasti. Ti se boje ili stide doći pred Isusa,

Scorched Bible remnant from the Bishop's Palace

of the United States who see a need and want to help in any way they can.

War should belong to the tragic past, to history. It shall find no place on humanity's agenda for the future.
—Pope John Paul II,
Homily at Coventry Cathedral, 1982

Medjugorje, my original inspiration to help the people of this beautiful country, became my spiritual home and base for delivering the humanitarian aid for the first few years.

*****

During my early solo visits, Gojko, a Croatian innkeeper who ran a bed-and-breakfast *pension* in Medjugorje, became one of my most reliable friends. He provided contacts to help transport supplies time and again from Split to Medjugorje and Mostar, about a 100-mile journey. He knew the Croatian army doctors and hospital staff, as well as the clinics in the area and their needs.

Gojko connected me to physicians in clinics, hospitals and refugee camps in nearby villages. These makeshift

Gojko and Jeanne McCue in Medjugorje (1993)

"camps," were set up in hotels, school gyms, and railroad cars to provide shelter for thousands of people.

Gojko also introduced me to Dr. Milenko, one of the first physicians I worked with. Dr. Milenko headed the medical team that cared for the wounded Croatian soldiers in the area. This was a war of citizen soldiers with few weapons. They made explosive devices out of soda cans, and bought their own rifles, bullets, and hand grenades. Many would leave the front lines, return home for a meal and a shower, and go back to the fighting.

Dr. Milenko was based between Mostar and Medjugorje, where an existing building was used as a staging area for supplies needed on the front. I would meet Dr. Milenko in Medjugorje and give him the supplies I brought: antibiotics,

Dr. Melinko and Jeanne McCue with supplies in Sarajevo

dressings, and small medical equipment, including blood pressure cuffs and portable EKG machines.

Each time I encountered Dr. Milenko, I asked what to bring on my next trip. On our first visit, he told me an ambulance was desperately needed to bring soldiers from the front line. An old station wagon was being used to transport the injured. I was traveling with my parish priest, who had brought along funds he had collected. He donated $1,000 to Dr. Melinko, who then purchased a used ambulance.

Gojko also introduced me to others who were helping in the war relief effort, including a friend in nearby Citluk who was a baker. He delivered bread in Mostar twice a week and invited me to help distribute to those in the bread lines. It was a common sight during war to see people standing in lines to gather provisions. They often risked their lives as they were subjected to constant shelling and sniper fire.

Once I came across a refugee lying listlessly on a mattress on the floor in a refugee camp. I gave him a pair of boots that had belonged to my son Daniel. I was gratified to be able to take a piece of my son's legacy and help another human being.

As part of the ethnic cleansing, not only churches, but also hospitals were targets and constantly exposed to destructive shelling by Serbian forces. Any institution that housed vital statistics was vulnerable. Hospitals were not immune.

In 1994, I was in a pediatric hospital distributing medical supplies and teddy bears when it began to be hit by mortar shells. The children did not flinch or cry, for they were used to attacks and bombs. Later, I learned that the

Maternity Hospital of Sarajevo had also been shelled, with many mothers and their infants among the causalities.

The Kosevo Hospital of Sarajevo was more than 150 years old and had just been remodeled in 1982. It, too, was shelled. During the war, this tertiary trauma hospital treated more than 8,000 wounded citizens and performed in excess of 12,000 operations. More than 1.2 million outpatients were treated in the hospital's clinics despite lack of supplies and equipment.

Even the hospital information system, which had vital statistics and patient data, was taken by the Yugoslav army. Trauma surgeons became experts in treatment of life-threatening injuries, working with scarce supplies. Rubber gloves and intravenous lines were reused.

During that time, the United Nations High Commission for Refugees (UNHCR) in Bosnia-Herzegovina provided food

Workers do laundry in the street at the Kosevo Hospital in Sarajevo

and water. Generators were used for power and hospital laundry was done manually by dedicated women using washboards.

Psychiatric hospitals offered mostly custodial care, and little therapy or treatment. I distributed hygiene kits that gave people the basic necessities.

In addition to personal articles, those first few years, I brought catheters, oxygen masks, aspirin, feeding tubes, drain sponges, infusion sets, and suction regulators. These items came from friends, relatives, and hospitals back home. I also brought such items as thermal underwear, toys, and hygiene items. I was a channel of the generosity of others.

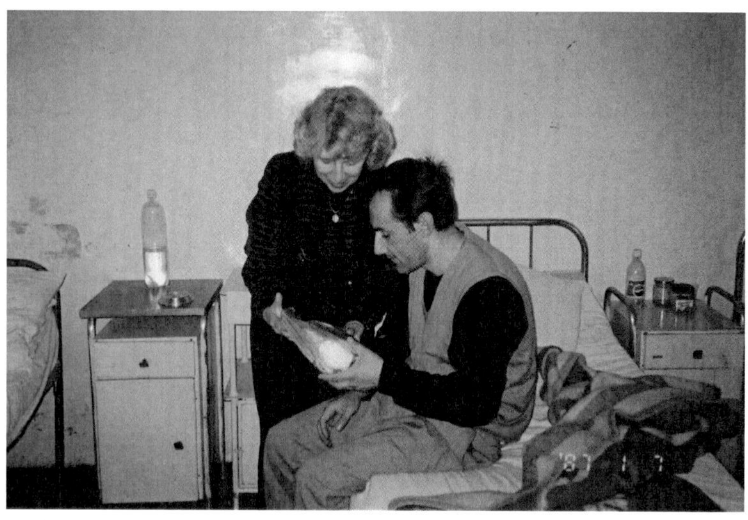

A psychiatric patient receives a hygiene kit at a hospital in Sarajevo

Constantly, I was reminded of the prayer of St. Francis of Assisi:

Make me a channel of your peace.
Where there is hatred let me bring your love.
Where there is injury, your pardon, Lord
And where there's doubt, true faith in you.
Oh, Master, grant that I may never seek
So much to be consoled as to console
To be understood as to understand
To be loved as to love with all my soul.

My hope was that I brought a message of generosity to these desperate people. Whenever we reach out to others, we promote peace.

An old woman on the streets of Medjugorje
offers bread as a way of thanks

During that first trip and on all subsequent trips delivering supplies, I experienced a grateful and unselfish people. Doctors would only take the supplies they needed. One little boy was given a toy and candy. He shared the sweets with his brother. An old woman eating bread in a park offered a piece to me.

During the early years of my missions, I met a third-grade school teacher, Vesna Rakic, in the town of Ljubuski, about 100 miles southeast of Split and the Adriatic coast. Ljubuski was a community of about 5,000, and home to another 3,000 refugees. At the school, there were about forty children in each class. My visit took place in winter, and the school had no heat whatsoever. The third-graders wore coats, the classrooms had no textbooks or composition books, few pencils, and the walls were bare. Teachers were paid $35 a month.

Vesna asked her students to make drawings of war and peace. Third-graders ought to be too young to know such things. But the horrors and atrocities were happening in their town and countryside. War planes zoomed overhead, there were constant air strikes, they heard the rumble of tanks and thud of mortars frequently, and saw the bodies of friends, relatives, and even parents being lowered into the ground. Their drawings showed the vivid reality of war and also hope of peace coming to their land. Their teacher wrote:

> *Every day we watch horrible things around us and we often think the world has forgotten us. It is encouraging to know that people on the*

> *other part of the world who don't even speak our language care about us. Today I am happy to see the faces of my children smiling, and that is because your love finds its way to their little hearts. In time, the pencils will be used and the books read, but the love & care we felt will stay forever in our hearts and minds. We appreciate your visits.*
>
> —Vesna

Vesna told me that the language of love is one that every human heart can understand. The children of Bosnia have always held a special place in my heart. I have always been amazed by their courage. Despite the burdens of war they had to endure, they smiled and hoped for better tomorrows.

I visited the school bringing supplies and gifts to the children. It was at this school that I started a pen pal

School children offer flowers as thanks for supplies and toys

Children in schools send hand-drawn pictures of war to pen pals in the US

exchange between her students and Milwaukee students. The letters were heart-wrenching, but at the same time uplifting and hopeful. It was gratifying to see the same generation talking even though they were worlds apart.

The children's drawings depicted not only planes dropping bombs and burning homes, but also images of peaceful homes with the sun, flowers and butterflies—signs of their hope. They dreamed of the day when peace would return to their devastated villages. The children of Bosnia had been cheated of their childhood and forced to grow up prematurely, focusing merely on survival.

One student in Wisconsin wrote:

Dear Pen Pal in Bosnia,

I am very sorry there is a war where you live . I wish there was something I could do to help. Cheering you would make me so happy. It must be hard for you right now. Right now we are studying peace in our class. We want to help you fight the war and be free. In my class we have pet salamanders Do you have any pets?

Love, Molly

Pictures drawn by the children in Ljubuski

Our gifts and letters from halfway across the world gave the children so much pleasure and showed them that people had not forgotten them. I received a letter from Vesna:

Jeanne,

We wish to thank you and all you and your friends doing for us (I do not speak English well)The life has changed in so many ways here. We haven't got the English teacher so I will try to express how I feel about your kindness and humanity.

I teach in an elementary school. Today I am happy to see the faces of my children smiling and that is because your love finds its way to their little hearts. We do appreciate you being around. Instead of my writing, there is one letter of one little girl in my class...

Dear Friends,
Thank you honestly for all gifts you send to me. All those little things I will share with my brother. He is younger than me and likes to draw. I hope there will be better times ahead when the war will be finished. Pray for me and for all little children in my country so they have happiest childhood, cause, just like other children in the world, we also dream about butterflies, songs, big parks, toboggans and a lot , a lot of sun and laughing.

God bless you (no name of girl)

Many journalists wrote about the impact of war on children. I remember one in particular who conveyed the shock of young children who heard planes zooming overhead, homes bursting into flames, and mortars exploding. These youngsters had vivid memories of friends and relatives being buried weekly as though it was commonplace.

Once, when I delivered several boxes of books and writing supplies, Vesna had the children prepare a skit for me. They wrote letters to the American children, which I took back home.

*****

For my first three trips, I was a solo humanitarian and traveled alone. After my work became known, columnist Bill Janz of the *Milwaukee Sentinel* and Father Bob Wells of my home parish accompanied me on my fourth trip. When I returned home from that trip, a five-part series by Bill was published in the Sentinel. It generated an outpouring of support. Tons of supplies were donated over the next 20 years.

> *Split, Croatia - For the third time this year, Jeanne McCue arrived here with more than her suitcase. She brought 2,000 pounds of medical equipment, candy, surgical masks, Cracker Jacks, hearing aids, and 3,000 dolls that she handed out one at a time to refugee kids.*

McCue was often followed by children, many of whom had only what she gave them. She was followed in refugee camps, on the street, in an orphanage, and in the dark in a large, former top-class hotel, where refugee children played soccer in the lobby.

While staying in this hotel where 700 refugees lived, McCue opened her door one night and found ten children lined up in the dark, waiting for anything she might give them. The hotel had no working elevators, no lights on the stairways, so the children climbed three flights in darkness and somehow found her door. If she hadn't had anything but paper clips, they probably would have accepted them with smiles and hugs.

McCue brought anesthesia kits, tracheal tubes, an Elvis tape, $10,000 worth of antibiotics, surgical gowns, cough drops, and 30 umbrellas packed in a case that looked so much as if it were holding rifles that we were stopped often by security guards who were worried what caliber the umbrellas were.

When McCue, who is a nursing supervisor at the Milwaukee County Medical complex, dropped off cases of baby formula at a clinic in a war zone in Bosnia-Herzegovina, she was applauded by nurses, who asked if she wanted them to type out what they called "a letter of thanksgiving."

> *"All I want is a hug," McCue said, and she hugged them.*
>
> *She is a prominent, extremely modest member of an unorganized army of private citizens who risk their lives and bring food, medicine, and clothing into areas in which the hatred is so thick that Muslims, Croats and Serbs spend much of their time trying to kill each other.*
>
> *Unpaid, unofficial humanitarians, many from Europe, bring supplies by plane, truck, van and car, and keep alive desperate people who have been repeatedly forgotten in this war.*
>
> *McCue has great speed and energy and when she bumps into something that bumps back, she bounces, reverses engines, and charges ahead. Nothing stops her but the clock, when it's time to go to church.*
>
> *—Milwaukee Sentinel, 1993*

On that fourth mission, I met a man named Jakob Durakovic, a wonderful man who headed Croatian Relief Services. He drove us to the Tomic Orphanage in Split, Croatia. As we entered, we noticed it was spotless and housed several rooms filled with babies who had been abandoned by their parents.

One boy, Jonathon, was ten months old and had been born with compromised limbs. The attendant told us he was scheduled for adoption by a couple in the United States, but he did not know the exact location. We spent a lot of time interacting with this wide-eyed and alert child. Jonathon would be receiving prostheses, but more importantly, he was getting new parents who wanted to raise him.

When the series was published in the *Milwaukee Sentinel*, Bill Janz received a call from a couple who lived a few hours away from Milwaukee. They told Bill they were convinced they were to be the adoptive parents! They told Bill that this would be the first time to view their son and asked for our photos.

As it turned out, they were indeed Jonathon's new parents. The day the article was published—November 9—was Jonathon's first birthday! Two months later, on a frigid January day, the couple brought him home.

Jonathon has grown into a healthy, independent, and successful young man. As a competitive swimmer, Jonathon holds multiple national records and is now a university student. I have seen him often through the years when he

Jeanne McCue and young friends
outside the Tomic orphanage in Split, Croatia

comes to Milwaukee to attend Croatian events. He is an inspiration about how someone cannot only survive, but thrive, when shown love and compassion.

The children of Bosnia hold a special place in my heart. Working to bring supplies and toys to them has been a gift from God. One cold November trip, I was accompanied by Bob Hiner. Bob was from Grand Rapids, Michigan. He had been with me on my first trip to that area with the southern relief agency. Bob became a one-man humanitarian mission in Michigan, bringing more than $6 million worth of supplies, including vans and cash to the people of that war-ravaged area. He also built a playground in Sarajevo in cooperation with the Croats, Muslims, and Serbs. The idea

Jeanne McCue at a Christmas party
for refugee children

Refugees lived in boxcars like these in Herzegovina during the war

Jeanne McCue visiting a refugee family at a refugee camp in Ljubuski (1993)

behind the playground was to promote healing in children of all nationalities.

Because of the war, many parents had lost employment and little money was available to feed the children. Bob and I decided to have a Christmas party for a large group of refugee children who were living in a hotel. Bob had brought Santa hats, and we played our roles with joy, bringing toys, books and clothes to these needy children.

Humanitarian aid should not only be measured in donations from generous people to those who are suffering. It should be measured in the goodwill that the donations bring. In years to come, the refugee children we help, regardless of ethnicity, will remember the acts of kindness they received from people they may never meet. The faces of those children inspired me to return again and again to bring help and hope to their lives. The grateful smiles of the children compelled me to continue.

Children are the world's most valuable resource and its hope for the future.
—John F. Kennedy

Hand-drawn art from children in Ljubuski tells the story of their life during the war

Chapter 4
The Early Years of Hope

We don't accomplish anything in this world alone, and whatever happens is the result of the whole tapestry of one's life and all the weavings of individual threads of one to another that creates something.
—Sandra Day O'Conner

I could spend a lifetime describing the people in Bosnia -Herzegovina who made all of these trips possible. Without them, I would have no contacts, no translators, no drivers, and no place to stay. After I made two trips with the southern mission group, I knew I would need people to meet me at the other end and help transport the thousands of pounds of cargo from the airport in Split to Medjugorje, Mostar, and later to Sarajevo. Gojko was that person.

I first met Gojko on my initial mission trip. He had a truck and spoke a little English. He lived with his wife and two children in Medjugorje and hosted pilgrimage groups at his pension. I was able to obtain his fax number and asked for help transporting supplies from Split to Medjugorie and Mostar.

For the next three years, Gojko would pick me up, negotiate the supplies through the ever-changing customs regulations, unload and load as many as 150 boxes of supplies to his truck, and drive us up the Croatian coast, through the Dalmatian mountains to Medjugorje.

We stored the boxes of supplies in his guesthouse. During the winter months, he had few, if any, pilgrim guests. So quite often, his pension had no heat or electricity. I remember washing my hair by candlelight in cold water, but that was how the people lived every day during this war.

Throughout my years working with him, Gojko was always reliable and had tremendous patience when shipments were delayed. He also had many contacts in the area, including the physicians on the front lines and hospitals, clinics, and refugee centers where aid was needed most.

Together, we would distribute supplies to medical and dental clinics, and to the hundreds of refugees who were living in all sorts of conditions—from luxury hotels transformed into refugee centers to schools to boxcars.

The most help was needed in Sarajevo, the city that had hosted the 1984 Winter Olympics. This beautiful city with cobblestone streets, churches, and restaurants, was filled with rich history and culture. It was nestled among snow-capped mountains with breathtaking scenery.

During the war, Sarajevo became the heart of darkness. Snipers killed innocent men, women, and children as they walked the streets to find a bread line. A young boy was shot in the face and killed as he held his mother's hand crossing the street. Ethnic cleansing had taken hold, and many women were taken to camps for the entertainment of

Serbian troops. Angelina Jolie's movie, *The Land of Blood and Honey,* is a poignant and terrifying look at these atrocities.

According to the *Survival Guide for Sarajevo,* author Suada Kapic instructed visitors and residents how to survive without transportation, hotels, taxis, telephones, food, shops, heating, water and electricity. Kapic begins the guide by stating:

> *This book was written at the site where one civilization was dismantled in the course of intentional violence, and where another one had to be born, the one of the 21st century. It is the picture of a civilization that emerges out of cataclysm, which makes something out of nothing, gives some messages for the future. Not because the future is necessarily a future of wars and disasters, but because humans are growing old and being born into a world which is ever less secure.*

The macabre guidebook was printed to help those stranded in Sarajevo with no means of escape. The book describes the places people now called home:

> *Those who were lucky still live in their apartments. Refugees and those whose apartments have been burned or destroyed by grenades are inhabiting the apartments of those who left Sarajevo before or during the war. Some enter the flats by breaking the doors and changing the locks. Windows are gone. destroyed by*

> *perpetual detonation. Some windows are protected by the lumber brought from the basement or roofs. Those homes are dark as graves. Bricks which can be found around destroyed buildings are used by those who still have walls and holes to fill. People accumulate their precious belongings in some corner of the apartment which they consider safest. Bathrooms are storage for paintings, photographs, documents, jewelry, and money.*

The book describes how water shortages lasted for days and weeks. People risked their lives waiting in lines to fill canisters. Electricity became almost nonexistent. The book warns that if people plan to come to the city, they must be prepared:

> *Bring good shoes which make you walk long and run fast, pants with many pockets, pills for water, Deutsche marks, batteries, matches, vitamins, canned food, drinks and cigarettes. Everything you bring will be consumed or exchanged for useful information. You should know when to skip a meal, how to turn trouble into a joke and be relaxed in impossible moments. Learn not to show emotions and don't be fussy about anything. Be ready to sleep in basements, eager to walk and work surrounded by danger. Give up all your former habits. Use the telephone when it works. Laugh when it doesn't. You'll laugh a lot. Despise, don't hate.*

During my first missions to Medjugorje and Mostar, I heard of the desperate needs of the people of Sarajevo from their friends, relatives, and physicians who had fled the besieged city. I longed to bring aid to these people, but a United Nations High Commission of Refugees (UNHCR) pass was needed, as well as a contact and military air transport.

According to a United Nations report at that time,

> *A total of 13,952 people were killed during the siege, including 5,434 civilians. The ARBiH suffered 6,137 fatalities, while Bosnian Serb military casualties numbered 2,241 soldiers killed. The 1991 census indicates that before the siege the city and its surrounding areas had a population of 525,980. There are estimates that prior to the siege the population in the city proper was 435,000. The current estimates of the number of persons living in Sarajevo range from between 300,000 to 380,000.*

On my way back to the United States in 1994, after my tenth mission to Medjugorje and Mostar, I met a man at the airport in Split who would change my life. Some people come into our lives and quickly go. Some stay a while, leaving footprints on our hearts, and we are never the same.

So it was for me after a chance meeting with Brother Thomas O'Grady from the St. John of God Order in Dublin, Ireland. Meeting this gracious man was one of the most meaningful coincidences I have ever experienced. Brother O'Grady became my contact to bring help and hope to the people of Sarajevo for years to come.

Brother O'Grady might never have stopped me if he had not seen a little shamrock I had in my luggage, which was opened by security on the airport floor. I dug through the contents of my suitcase, trying to find the item that was setting off the security scanner.

Brother O'Grady walked past and asked in his cheerful Gaelic accent. "Would you be Irish?" I explained that my heritage was German, but I had an Irish surname. He introduced himself as a religious brother working with Refugee Trust of Ireland. He had established programs in war-torn Sarajevo for the elderly, blind, traumatized children, and the mentally challenged.

During our brief conversation, he offered to be my contact, and would arrange for me to obtain a UNHCR Field Monitor pass to fly to Sarajevo on a UN Army transport plane the following February.

Brother O'Grady was part of the International Refugee Trust (IRT). This is an organization established by Father Kevin Doheny in Ireland in 1989, the year of my son Daniel's death. He established the organization to create awareness of the terrible injustices in war-torn countries and the recognition that we all have a part to play in striving to eliminate this suffering.

Brother O'Grady had worked as a missionary in Africa since 1967. His work continued on a greater scale with the creation of the IRT, a network of support groups around the world. One of those networks was in Ireland. The IRT continues to work in Uganda, South Sudan, Thailand, and Jordan. Conflicts in Syria are now forcing hundreds of thousands of people to flee into neighboring Europe has created further need for this kind of aid.

The IRT's vision is to imagine a world "where all people live peacefully in the place they call home, with the skills, opportunities and confidence to support themselves and progress socially and economically."

When the Balkan war began, the Irish branch of IRT organized convoys of food, blankets, and medical supplies by road directly to Bosnia. They used the Franciscan fathers to do the distribution. In 1993, Brother O'Grady volunteered his services. The IRT in Bosnia developed rehabilitation programs for the visually impaired and blind. They work with senior citizens, the intellectually disabled and traumatized children. When Brother O'Grady first opened an office in Split, he visited interior villages and penetrated into Sarajevo. He was invited by then-Archbishop Vinco Puljic to set up programs in Sarajevo.

Refugee Trust staff and interpreter Ana-Marija Lasic.
Seated (L to R): Jeanne McCue, Brother O' Grady and Dinko.

Brother O'Grady and I met only seven months after he established his programs in Sarajevo. By that time, he had made an impact on the city and won the hearts of those he served. He worked in cooperation with the ministries of Bosnia-Herzegovina, with 60 international non-governmental organizations (NGOs) operating during the war in Sarajevo. He lived among the people in Sarajevo and suffered shortages of water, electricity and gas, as well as continuous shelling and sniper attacks.

He also linked refugees in Ireland with relatives in Sarajevo, providing his own mail system to let loved ones know their relatives were safe. During the war, he drove truckloads of aid from Ireland to Bosnia under extremely difficult conditions.

Peace is deciding to live together again.
—A sign at an IRT office in Bosnia

I recalled this profound message on a trip in 2015 when I visited two goat farmers near the town of Travnik, Bosnia-Herzegovina. They were neighbors and their families had lived there for generations. We had donated goats to both families—one Muslim, the other Bosnian Christian.

When I think of all the conflict and how much effort it will take to heal the wounds, I recall the two farmers in the field in front of me, on a scenic mountain on a sunny day in September, discussing their herds. They were living again together in peace.

In a letter I received from him not too long ago, Brother O'Grady looked back and remembered all that had happened during those early years. He wrote:

> *I remember you saying 'I want to get to Sarajevo with some donations'. I think that was the day Our Lady linked you up with me and so began your journey to Sarajevo. Look at all the work and love you have provided for so many and the care and concern you had for them. Yes, that is servicing and loving Christ. Thank God for you and all your friends. You have, without knowing it or being aware of it, been building up the Body of Christ the Church all this time."*
>
> —Brother Thomas O'Grady
> May 30, 2013

Jeanne McCue and Father Anton Jelic at a goat farm in Travnik, Bosnia

At a recent reunion with Brother O'Grady in Dublin, he and I recounted the many missions I made thanks to his assistance. He is a humble man with a giving spirit and a tendency to minimize all of the work he carried out during those dangerous times. We spoke about the efficacy and obstacles of providing humanitarian aid in a war zone.

He recalled spending much of his time making sure that the charities and the beneficiaries of the aid were legitimate. It was important to reassure both our Irish and American donors that their funds and donations directly reached those most in need.

> *Everything that is given to Jeanne goes directly to the people; there is no middle man. This caused donors to multiply because they knew that they were making a difference in the most direct way possible.*
> —Peg Masterson Edquist, co-author and niece of Jeanne McCue

Bringing Hope in a Box

Transporting tons of humanitarian aid to a country at war and a city under siege at first seemed like a monumental and daunting task. I started with the Yellow Pages—looking for an air cargo company that would transport shipments of aid to Split via Frankfurt, Germany. I found Lufthansa Airlines in Chicago.

On the receiving end, I always found reliable partners during the war in Bosnia and Sarajevo to work with me to receive the aid and negotiate the air freight through the ever-changing rules of customs. For the first three years, that partner was Gojko.

Later, Brother O'Grady was the vital link I needed to send and distribute aid directly to Sarajevo. Without the import number assigned to all NGOs, I could never have gotten my donations through customs. Brother O'Grady made me a Refugee Field Monitor, which allowed me to enter the city. He facilitated shipments at first by truck from Split to Sarajevo via the UN Blue Road, the only land route open during the siege.

The IRT had a multidisciplinary team of a social worker, a psychologist, nurses, a physician and home helpers. They visited the often-immobile elderly in high-rise apartments without electricity or heat on the front lines of Sarajevo.

While the guns of conflict echoed and snipers tried to control the crossroads, the IRT team went on with their daily rounds of caring for the 1,400 elderly people living in District 1. I often accompanied Brother O'Grady on the visits and returned home with renewed energy and determination to continue the missions.

It was gratifying to witness firsthand the distribution of our aid going directly to the most needy. My photos provided vivid documentation to share with generous donors at home. Refugee Trust gave them hope and strength for the future.

The generosity and caring of others has been channeled through me and I feel privileged to play that role. Refugees who fled to the United States often contacted me to be a courier for letters, cash, and small packages to loved ones they had to leave behind.

A couple from Maryland read of my missions in 1995 in a national Catholic magazine. They were hosting a young Bosnian refugee who had fled Sarajevo during the war. His mother died in the conflict and his father had recently taken his own life. His sisters fled to Macedonia. His parents' neighbors had saved the parents' photo albums and jewelry. He requested that I bring them back and take pictures of his parents' graves. His host mother wrote:

> *Dear Jeanne,*
>
> *Thank you for helping our Bosnian boy keep in touch with his home town. It breaks my heart to see him so down. And hopefully he will feel better soon.*
>
> *Jill*

On my next trip in November 1995, Dino, one of our drivers, helped me locate the apartment—on the 10th floor of a high rise in the District 1, where Brother O'Grady had projects for the elderly. The electricity and elevators were not working, so we trudged up ten dark flights to the apartment of their Serbian neighbors, who were keeping the personal effects of the boy's parents.

I carried the items with me on the flight back home. The young man was overjoyed when he received his family's treasures and could hardly express his gratitude.

One of the most interesting and gracious families I met was that of our driver, Dino. His brother-in-law was the driver for Refugee Trust. Dino lived in a 15th-floor apartment with his wife, who was a physician, his father-in-law, Hazim, and a young toddler son. He invited me to stay with his family during my 1997 mission.

Hazim was in his 60s and had been a gymnast who competed in the 1960 Olympics in Rome. He delighted in showing me every morning how many push-ups he could do. The apartment had no running water, so we could not bathe. One evening, to my surprise, Hazim led me to the bathroom to show a tub partially filled with warm water. He had made multiple trips in the small elevator with buckets of water to the 15th floor. He heated the water on a gas burner in the tiny kitchen. I will never forget his hospitality.

One evening, I told Hazim how I loved to dance. He found some polka music and we danced around the small living room. I had never dreamed that I would be dancing with an Olympic gymnast in a war zone. My mourning had turned to dancing!

There is a time for everything and a season
for every activity under heaven—
a time to mourn and a time to dance."
—Ecclesiastes 4

A Bosnian grandmother had settled in Milwaukee for medical care, leaving behind her family in Zenica. She asked me to bring her daughter letters, money and gifts for her granddaughters and appreciated the photos I brought back to her.

The Blue Road

For the two years leading up to my first trip to Sarajevo, Bosnia and Herzegovina had been exposed to a brutal assault by Serbian forces and had suffered over 200,000 deaths. More than 1.5 million people had been displaced from their homes—many forced to disperse to all corners of the world. Bosnia was in a death grip, while Europe and the international community did little to help.

At home in America, I saw images of carnage and suffering in the daily newspaper and on the news program *Nightline* on ABC. It was frightening to see but later, when I was bringing aid, I had no fear.

Sarajevo was totally sealed off from outside entry and aid. During the first few years of the war, 75 percent of all food and assistance came through the airport. By 1994, the city was closed to all humanitarian traffic. The only official route was the United Nations' "Blue Road," which would become a lifeline for humanitarian aid. It also was the route I would use to bring needed supplies to the city.

This road led to Mount Igman, which during peacetime had been the site of several events of the 1984 Olympics. During the war, French UN forces had to blast an open passage along precipitous cliffs to prepare a route for convoys of food, medical supplies, and other humanitarian aid. Hundreds of aid organizations transported essential items over the Blue Road from the Adriatic coast into Sarajevo. The first shipment I sent to Brother O'Grady from Split was transported via the Blue Road.

On my second mission to Sarajevo, I experienced this rough and treacherous mountain route. During the winter of 1995, Bob Hiner and I were picked up by Brother O'Grady in an ancient Mitsubishi. The cold wind was strong and I tried to keep warm inside the battered van.

The gravel road had no pavement or guardrails and was very narrow. When a truck came toward us from Sarajevo, we had to move to the edge of the cliff to make room. Under icy conditions, the van crawled up the slippery mountain with a slow hum, shifting when it hit a pothole or when Admir, our driver, swerved to avoid a damaged section of road.

We had been traveling toward Sarajevo for about 30 minutes when Admir edged out to avoid a truck coming our way. In seconds, we were stuck in snow and ice on the edge of an icy cliff. I sucked in a cold breath of air and listened while Brother O'Grady spoke with Admir. Bob and Brother O'Grady got out of the car while Admir stayed behind the wheel. We tried to determine how to free ourselves without the vehicle going over the cliff.

The only solution was to get out and push. The narrow road left little space for two cars, let alone two men pushing a van. I sat in the frigid air, focused on slowing my heart rate, closed my eyes, and prayed to get us through. After what seemed like an eternity, the men freed the van and we were back on the road.

The Tunnel of Hope

Another unofficial supply and exit route was the Sarajevo Tunnel of Hope. The high mountains surrounding the Bosnian capital of Sarajevo made it easy for enemies to encircle and easily cut off the city from the rest of the world. Serb forces did this during the siege from 1992 to 1995. Trapped citizens came under incessant bombardment for three and a half years with no way in or out of the town except across the airport runway. Many attempting the run lost their lives to snipers. Supplies dwindled to nearly nothing.

The Bosnian army and volunteers decided to dig a tunnel under the airstrip. The location was kept secret as

A souvenir postcard shows the Tunnel of Hope in Sarajevo

the Bosnian army and volunteers began to excavate using picks and shovels. Four months later, on July 30, 1993, the 800-meter (about 2,400 feet) passage was ready.

In the next two years, between 4,000 and 5,000 people used the tunnel to ferry supplies, weapons, and the injured in and out of Sarajevo. Brother O'Grady once accompanied a paralyzed boy out for medical treatment. The Tunnel of Hope became a lifeline for the people of Sarajevo.

I sought out the Tunnel of Hope in 2009, when Maja, one of my interpreters, told me it had been transformed into a museum. From the outside, it looked like an average house. Once inside, the tunnel could be seen in the main room. It was coarsely made, about six feet high, with some electricity to provide light as people passed through. My thoughts and prayers went to Brother O'Grady and the many other heroic people who attempted to transport patients, bring in supplies, and help others escape.

The worst of these times came to a slow ebb in 1996, just after the Dayton Peace Accord. But things in Sarajevo were not the same. The impacts of the war were stark and tangible. They continue to this day. Broken buildings line the streets of Sarajevo. Broken marriages will forever be divided by ethnic hate. Broken women were sexually brutalized, and they, along with their families, seek to rebuild their lives.

National Geographic magazine chronicled the effects of war with shocking statistics. Since the war began, it stated that 60,000 NATO-led peacekeeping troops from more than 30 nations, including 20,000 from the U.S., had been dispatched to separate the combatants—giving Serbs,

Croats, and Muslims a chance to recover from the worst atrocities and destruction in Europe since WW II. From a population of 4.3 million Bosnians in 1991, 200,000 were now dead; 200,000 more were injured, including 50,000 children. More than 2.5 million Bosnians had been driven from their homes. Sixty percent of the houses in Bosnia, half of the schools, and a third of the hospitals had been razed or damaged. Power plants, roads, and water systems lay in ruins. Fields and vineyards were abandoned, rivers were contaminated by toxic wastes from bombed-out industrial plants. The soil was polluted with millions of leg-shattering land mines.

This world was so different than mine, and yet I was drawn to go there again and again. My most challenging trip to Sarajevo was on the horizon. It couldn't come soon enough.

Chapter 5
Sarajevo: The Saddest City in the World

In February 1995, I spent a week in the Medjugorie/ Mostar area. Then it was time to go on to Sarajevo, known then as the "saddest city in the world.." Before I was to leave on my first mission to Sarajevo, Gojko warned me not to go. He kept repeating "*Ne, ne! Boomba boomba.*" ("No! No! Bombs! Bombs!") I appreciated his concern, but went anyway.

Word spread quickly through Medjugorje that I was leaving for Sarajevo. Almost immediately, refugees who had fled from Sarajevo wanted me to take little packages to their families. A woman physician gave me a small paper bag with new underwear for her elderly mother. My delivery of those items meant so much to people who had no other way to communicate with loved ones.

Gojko drove me to Split, where my journey to Sarajevo would begin. Brother O' Grady had instructed me to find the UNHCR on Diakom Farm Road on the outskirts of town. I left my bags with friends and walked a few miles to the office. Once there, I showed my passport and signed the necessary documents to receive my UNHCR field monitor pass. That first step allowed me to gain access to besieged Sarajevo.

As a nurse and a grandmother from Wisconsin, I could hardly believe that I had the privilege of going to the front lines of a war to help others.

Brother O'Grady told me to wait in a Split hotel coffee shop for a man named Dinko. Brother O'Grady had not described the person I was going to meet. Soon after I arrived, a tall young man approached me carrying a white flak jacket and helmet. That was Dinko. He introduced himself in fluent English. We were to leave the Split airport on the UN plane within an hour. The bulky, protective gear was for me!

Within a few minutes, we were on the tarmac with UN soldiers and a few reporters, plus some dogs sniffing bags for explosives. I carried only a small backpack and donned the white flak jacket for the flight. I was about to enter a world of unknowns—of conflict and massive human

Jeanne McCue on the tarmac at the airport during her first visit to Sarajevo in 1995.

Signs in the Sarajevo airport

Jeanne McCue and her driver Dinko inside a United Nations transport plane

suffering. Despite these tense surroundings, I had no fear. God was with me, as always.

We clambered into the plane and were told to sit on a long plank fastened to the wall of the cargo plane. The only other passengers were soldiers and reporters. I was the only woman. As we approached the Sarajevo airport, I saw a burned-out plane on the tarmac. This truly was a war zone.

Once we landed, Dinko told me to put on my helmet and informed me that we would get a "shuttle" into Sarajevo. It was a cold, snowy day and I looked around for our transport. All I could see was a gray United Nations armored tank. I quickly realized the tank *was* our shuttle.

I followed Dinko to the tank and climbed up the side of the immense vehicle toward the hatch opening. The tank was manned by French UN soldiers, and the air inside was

Inside the United Nations transport plane;
Jeanne McCue's first trip to Sarajevo

thick with tobacco smoke. The soldiers wore small blue flak jacket vests. I was envious of how snug those vests looked on the weary soldiers. I made a mental note to buy one when I got home.

As I descended the ladder into the tank, the soldiers made comments in French. With a loud clanking, we started to move. After about 20 minutes, the tank came to a stop. Dinko told me that it was the end of our ride. When we climbed out, it looked like we were in the middle of nowhere.

By now, it was mid-afternoon. We watched the tank pull away. Dinko told me to wait by the side of the road. He would try to find a ride to take us into the city. Then, he

Jeanne McCue near a street sign in Sarajevo warning of snipers

looked up into the mountains and told me, "Serbs are up there." I knew he meant snipers were in the hills. I did not want to be a target and so I removed my white flak jacket.

I had no idea where we were or how long it would take to get into the city. My well-being and trust were placed in a young man I had met only hours earlier. During my wait for his return, I had time to reflect on the events that led me to this narrow, lonely road.

Thinking of the hours and days ahead, I wondered what I would witness. Would I witness the images I had seen on the news? I thought of World War II and how the world had said, "Never again" to massacres and ethnic cleansings of innocent people. But it was happening in this country and the city I was about to enter.

Death notices were nailed to trees in most of Bosnia during the war

About half an hour later, Dinko returned with an elderly man driving an old, battered Yugo. It was dusk when we drove slowly into Sarajevo.

As it turned out, Sarajevo was also a city I would grow to love and return to again and again. Despite the obvious danger, a feeling of peace enveloped me. I knew God had brought me here and would protect me.

The air was thick with smoke and particles. Abandoned, burned-out cars lined the streets, which were littered with debris. Garbage was piled up high near buildings. Light poles with no lights leaned precariously over streets full of potholes from the shelling. The few people I saw outside scurried to their homes or destinations with plastic water jugs and loaves of bread under their arms. I peered out the

A blind man walks the streets of Sarajevo

Yugo's dirty windows and saw a blind man trying to find his way home.

All places of worship—the Catholic churches and cathedrals, mosques, and even the Gozi Husrev Beg Mosque in Old Town—had been partially or fully destroyed by Serbian shelling. The post office, a three-story structure on the Miljacka River, had been turned to rubble. As we drove slowly, Dinko told me that cultural and historical buildings were targeted, even the National Library, which was filled with ancient documents. Many Sarajevo residents braved heavy sniper fire and formed a human chain to save precious pieces of history after the library was bombarded.

We passed a cemetery and saw fresh graves everywhere. Funerals were held in the early morning or at dusk for safety. Death notices were nailed to trees and the sides of buildings. The notices were bordered in green if the deceased was Muslim, black if the person had been Christian. The dead were buried in parks and a large sports

Apartment building destroyed by shelling in Sarajevo

A view of the countryside from a bombed-out building in Mostar

stadium because most of the cemeteries were full. Some of the dead were buried near homes, next to mosques or playgrounds.

Sarajevo had been under siege for three years when I first visited. Survival was not easy for people under such circumstances, but I met and became friends with those who had chosen to stay and endure the suffering. The hardships of war were evident on their weary, worried faces. Many Serbs faced the same deprivation as their Muslim and Croat neighbors. They fought bravely in the Bosnian army against the Serb military and were called Chetniks.

My Friends in Sarajevo

It was dark when our driver brought us to Brother O'Grady's Refugee Trust apartment office on Ferhadija Street in Sarajevo. He and his staff welcomed me. We had Irish tea and crackers. I was introduced to a young student, Ana-Marija Lasic, who offered to be my interpreter.

Brother O'Grady had asked Cardinal Vinko Pulic if I could stay with a Catholic family during my visit. He suggested the Lasic family. On my first and second trips, I stayed in their apartment.

Ana-Marija lived there with her family. She told me it had been her parents' home throughout their married life. She and her brother Ivan had attended the Catholic school across the street. I was invited into their home and hearts and was able to listen to so many of their heartbreaking stories.

We set off for her family's apartment up the dark winding streets of Sarajevo. The air was thick with particles from the constant shelling. Her family's home was in an old apartment building in which they had lived for more than 20 years. We climbed the wide marble steps to her second-floor apartment, where I was warmly greeted by her parents, Marija and Sylvester, her brother Ivan, Aunt Ina, Grandmother Lasic, and their Muslim neighbors, who were eager to meet the courageous American nurse who had ventured into their city.

They offered strong coffee and were eager to relate stories of hardship and struggles, as well as those of survival and endurance. I heard how they risked their lives standing in bread lines and carrying buckets of water back to the apartment. Ana-Marija's family also talked of spending hours in candlelit cellars with neighbors during bombing raids. They said they felt imprisoned. Ivan said he dreamed of eating an egg, something he had not done since the war began.

Prices were out of reach for most foods—a single banana cost around $6. Ana-Marija said her brother would often look at cookbooks, and imagine he was eating the food in the pictures.

Although I had arrived utterly exhausted near midnight, we talked for nearly two hours. Then, Ana-Marija led me to the apartment of a businessman who had fled Sarajevo. I found a bed and collapsed to the sound of mortar shells exploding outside my window.

That was the place I would call home for the next three days. Several months later, Ana-Marija wrote to me:

> *April 30, 1995*
>
> *Dear Ms. Jeanne,*
>
> *We received mail you sent us. Thank you so much for photos and everything. Unfortunately situation is getting worse every day. People get killed and injured of sniper fire & shells. Sometimes I wonder how we will survive shelling and destroying again. I'm as everybody, very scared. I simply cannot understand it. But faith in God gives us a lot of courage and supports us.*

This Easter was (and still is) a beautiful and great experience. I think about Jesus and his sacrificing and dying for all of us. I rejoice because he loves us and will never leave us. It does not matter what we look like as long as there is forgiveness in our hearts.

We all hope you will soon be here with us and that situation will be better. We miss you very much and we think of you all the time.
You showed us that ordinary people in the world care about us.

With love,
Ana-Marija, Silvo, Ivan, Marija
and Grandmother

July 10, 1995

Dear Ms. Jeanne,

I guess you came to Bosnia as you promised. It is too dangerous here in Sarajevo.

I am so sorry I could not see you. We will meet in a better and safer time. Every day at least one person gets killed of shell or sniper. Doesn't matter and sometimes it is a bit horrifying when you hear things like that on news and you think Thank God it is not me.. That is cruel and selfish I know but it is reality. That is our life, though it does not look like one.

> *We are all struggling to say normal, sincerely. I doubt that anyone will be normal when all this comes to an end. We have no running water, no gas for months. We get electricity every 4 or 10 days. Everything is very expensive. You cannot imagine to live without running water, gas and electricity. Don't even try to imagine. I wish this never happens again to anyone.*
>
> *Only real oasis of peace, happiness and real love is our church and my friends – Community of Sacred Cross. I go on low mass and listen to words of Old and New Testament, when I get Holy Communion I know that God loves me and will never leave me alone. I wonder why people can't see that the only way to live and be loved – is to love. In all sacraments, in the Holy Bible and many other things I can see only love, God's love, Many people don't want to see.*
>
> *Anything, anywhere – that is very sad. I hope to see you very soon. When you come again, Ivan will be in Seminary in Zadar.*
>
> *Love, Ana-Marija & Family*

After our night of conversation, I awoke to a cup of wonderful Bosnian coffee. Soon we were off to the cathedral for 8 o'clock mass. Then we started our busy day.

Brother O'Grady and I attended the NGO Council Meeting at the Chamber of Commerce. The council assisted in coordination of international aid. International NGOs in Sarajevo held weekly meetings to update everyone on the progress of aid, development, and security. About 40 people from all over the world attended the meeting. Brother O'Grady introduced me as the International Refugee Trust (IRT) representative from the United States. We made visits to the IRT projects in Sarajevo to assess the needs.

At this time, the elderly in Sarajevo lived in apartments with no services, so they were unable to find food or medical care. IRT provided soup, bread and basic medical care. We visited a diabetic woman, one of 1,400 elderly and disabled who lived in District 1 of Sarajevo. She lived in a third-floor apartment as a bed-ridden amputee. Her face lit up when she saw us.

We then made a home visit to a middle-aged former businessman who was blind and paralyzed from a shrapnel injury to his head. He lived in an apartment with windows covered in plastic provided by the UNHCR.

The blind felt isolated and helpless during the war. They had to move to unfamiliar surroundings and much of their special equipment had been destroyed by fires and shelling. The normally routine task of collecting rations and water was fraught with danger.

We also visited many of the developmentally disabled, including a family with 15-year-old twins who had not been out of their apartment in three years.

During my subsequent visits, we toured a war hospital located underground a shelter to protect patients from the constant shelling. The shelter was divided into "containers," which served specific surgical or medical needs, including delivery room, an operating room, or patient ward.

The medical director explained how limited supplies were because of restricted movement. This makeshift

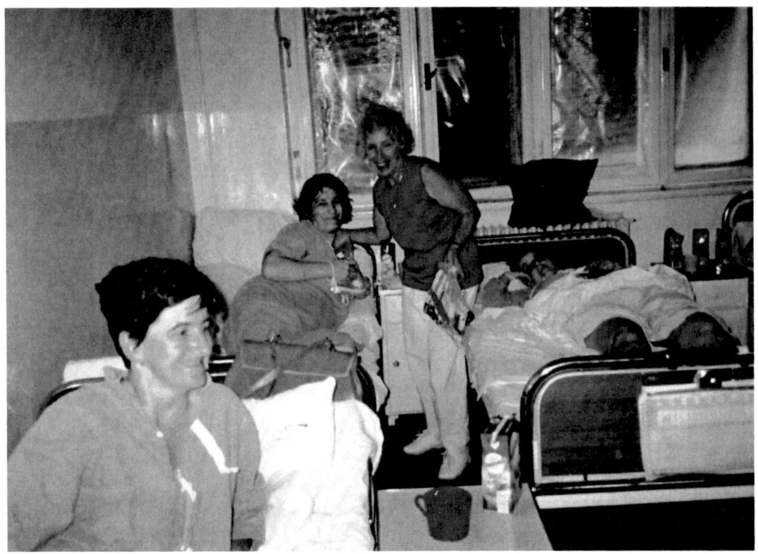

Jeanne McCue distributing mommy/baby packs to women in the obstetrics ward at a Mostar hospital

hospital had been scheduled to be built for a small Bosnian town called Zenica near Sarajevo, but was sent to Mostar because of the urgent need.

An orthopedic physician I met pleaded for Penrose drains—soft tubes used to drain wounds after operations—for three patients with amputations. He explained that their amputation sites were not healing and the patients could not be fit for prostheses.

I also went into the obstetric department to bring mommy/baby packs, handmade quilts, and medical supplies.

Brother O'Grady, Ana-Marija and I next toured a pediatric clinic. The clinic had one dedicated pediatrician who worked for the IRT as a general practitioner.

The only in-patient room in the hospital, more like a clinic, had three beds standing side to side filled with injured children. I rushed back to our car to retrieve teddy bears and saw the children's eyes light up when I got back with the toys.

A psychiatric hospital in a shelter had no windows and 24 patients in one room. I handed out hygiene packs to them and they were so grateful.

Small pockets of need were everywhere. An orphanage had been destroyed in the war and was being rebuilt. When it was up and running, I brought school supplies, blankets, and hygiene products. The facility, Egipat, had been damaged by constant shelling during the four years of war and subsequent fires. It stood vacant at the time of our first visit.

Brother O'Grady introduced me to Sister Liberia of the Handmaids of the Baby Jesus. The sisters of her order had educated and cared for orphan children of all nationalities since the orphanage had been built more than a century before. The House was established in 1899 by the first Archbishop of Sarajevo, Josip Stadler, who entrusted the orphanage to the sisters. The name "Egipat" is the Croatian word for Egypt and comes from a passage in the gospel:

> *When they had departed behold, the angel of the Lord appeared to Joseph in a dream and said, "Rise, take the child and Mary his mother, flee to Egypt and stay there until I tell you. Herod is going to search for the child and*

> *destroy him. Joseph took the child and his mother by night and departed to Egypt.*
> —Matthew 2: 13-15

The name symbolized the vigilance by some people to protect the innocent refugees against the assault of evil. Shortly after World War II in 1948, the Communist regime expelled the sisters, took the children away, and confiscated the property. For 47 years, the sisters pleaded with the local authorities for permission to resume their activity of caring for orphan children.

On Christmas Eve, 1995, during the time in history when the Holy Family sought refuge in Egypt, news came of the signing of the Dayton Peace Treaty. The next week, local authorities gave permission to the Handmaids to return and start repairing the damage to the building.

Jeanne McCue with a Roma refugee child in Sarajevo (1995)

Restoration was finished within months and today, happy children are cared for by the sisters. For the past 15 years, I have brought aid to Egipat, providing shoes, vitamins, handmade quilts, teddy bears, dental supplies and milk money.

My Bosnia Family Extends its Arms

Brother O'Grady's IRT was crucial in those early years. It linked me to the programs active in Sarajevo and brought the bulk of my aid to the organization.

When Brother O'Grady left in 1997 due to health concerns, I worked with his secretary, who continued to make connections and let me know where to deliver donations. The secretary's sister became my interpreter and worked with me for eight years. She took care of my appointments and arranged everything for many years. She was a wealth of knowledge and explained the culture and background of this complex country.

In the ensuing years, I worked with dozens of drivers and interpreters. I met them through past connections and they became my lasting friends.

Before he left, Brother O'Grady also introduced me to two Irish nuns, Sister Rosaleen and Sister Anne, from the order of the Sisters of the Cross and Passion in Ireland. Great need existed to start a home hospice program for poor patients with cancer who could not leave their homes. I started to bring financial aid and supplies, as well as educational manuals about caring for the dying that I received from palliative care doctors in America. The workers began to teach nurses and hold seminars to give end-of-life care in Sarajevo and other parts of Bosnia.

When I returned to Wisconsin, a home health company called to say they had supplies to give to my missions. The Irish sisters' first home hospice, NJEGA, had its grand opening in October 1999. I brought aid to this hospice ever since and have gone on home care visits with their doctors and nurses.

The sisters had to overcome many obstacles. A rule stated that only a doctor could administer narcotics for pain outside the hospital. This was not possible in palliative home care. The sisters managed to change that rule so nurses could administer the drugs. Eventually, they opened inpatient hospices in Sarajevo and Tuzla.

Jeanne McCue with refugee children in Bonovici, Bosnia

The Transport of Hope

Because I needed to find new ways to reach refugees, the sisters told me about Save the Children (STC) in the United Kingdom. STC is a worldwide organization that helps children. Whenever you hear about a disaster, STC is there. The UK and American STC had offices in Bosnia. The sisters were more familiar with the UK STC, so I worked with that organization.

The sisters also told me about refugees in Tuzla, a small town about 2½ hours' drive from Sarajevo. STC Sarajevo received my supplies from customs and transported them to Tuzla and the settlements. Tuzla was home to many refugees, including survivors of a massacre in the neighboring town of Srebrenica in July 1995, along with Roma refugee children.

At the height of the war, Serb troops overran what had been declared a United Nations Safe Zone protected by Dutch and UN peacekeeping forces. Despite the supposed protection, Serbian forces invaded and told the women that they were taking the men and boys to a camp. Instead, the troops slaughtered up to 8,000 Muslim men and boys. Many were killed in a school gymnasium, others in a football field. Some were forced to dig their own mass graves.

Many publications wrote about these atrocities, including the *Christian Science Monitor,* one of whose reporters won a Pulitzer Prize for coverage of the war. Among the articles were criticisms of the war's safe zones, many of which had been turned into areas of mass graves. One article told how the international community partially disarmed thousands of men and then delivered them to their sworn enemies to be murdered. The articles condemned the fall of Srebrenica, which left thousands of corpses, and as many children without fathers, grandfathers, uncles and brothers.

To this day, many women do not know the fate of their husbands, sons, or fathers. The International War Crimes Tribunal continues to exhume mass graves and identify remains through DNA.

Srebrenica was left in shambles. The survivors traveled to Tuzla, where they lived in the makeshift camps of Grab Potok and Bonovici. When I first visited Tuzla in 2001, it consisted of several settlements on the outskirts of the city. Families lived in one or two rooms in large barracks. In these bleak surroundings, I encountered mostly older men, women, and young children. Some mothers lived in a single room with their children. In winter there was no heat. Because the barracks were far from the city, the children had to walk to school in Tuzla. I brought warm boots, mittens, school bags and other school supplies, which were gratefully accepted.

While I was visiting, the refugees would line up to have me take a Polaroid picture of them so they would have some documentation of their existence. All had fled their homes and had no records or identification. Mothers cherished the instant photos of their remaining children. It was the best gift I could give them.

Among other supplies I sent to Tuzla, were toiletries, hats, and winter shoes. During that time, I sent my biggest shipment ever, 40 forty boxes of supplies that had been packaged and prepared by me and my friends, nicknamed the "Muffins."

Jeanne McCue with supplies ready to ship
from her home in Wisconsin

Save the Children in Sarajevo let me use its registration information to get through customs. Because it was a large and established NGO, I could get supplies through without much red tape. Once in Bosnia, STC transported my supplies to Tuzla and the settlement camps. I could not have done this without STC.

For a shipment in December, 2001, I decided to put my son Daniel's new wool jacket at the top of the box. It was given to Aldin, a young boy whose family had been refugees from Kosovo. Aldin was an insulin-dependent diabetic. I was touched that he had received the coat. I met Aldin's family and brought funds to him via STC for many years. STC staff members remain dear friends of mine.

After a few years, STC directed me to the needs of the Roma children in Zavidovici. Each year, I try to bring the Roma children funds so they can go to school with supplies and have health exams before they go. Hepatitis and sickness are rampant in Roma communities, where no money is available to pay for the health exams. I give money to STC, which is then passed on to the Roma people, with thorough documentation of where the funds are distributed.

In 2005, I connected with another charitable organization, The Bread of St. Anthony. While staying with the

Above: The Bread of St. Anthony operated one of the largest soup kitchens in Sarajevo during the war

Below: People waiting in line at the soup kitchen

Franciscan Sisters of Provare Street, a priest named Father Stipan Radic came to say mass. After the service, he learned that I was bringing aid. He asked if I could come to a soup kitchen run by The Bread of St. Anthony, which he headed.

Father Stipan ran an organization that helped the poor and elderly in Sarajevo. His soup kitchen fed more than 900 people of all religious and ethnic origins each day. The organization also provided home visits by nurses for bed-ridden elderly who had no relatives to care for them. The Bread of St. Anthony also offers food and clothing for refugees from other countries so they can resettle in their homes with dignity.

I was excited to find a new connection to get supplies into Sarajevo. I sent blankets, toys, vitamins, and other items for those who were touched by Father Stipan's programs.

Each time I traveled to Sarajevo, I gave Father Stipan him a monetary donation for the soup kitchen. Because The Bread of St. Anthony had a customs number, I was able to send supplies through the organization. A Wisconsin woman had been making colorful quilts for me for years, but it was hard to distribute them in large numbers. Father Stipan accepted the quilts, got them through customs, and delivered them to his programs and the Egipat Children's Home.

People I met along the way continued to help me find the needy. A woman in Sarajevo contacted me ten years after I worked with Catholic Relief Services. She told me about diabetic children who lived in Zavidovic. Most were without proper supplies to help them manage the disease.

When I started going to Zavidovic in 2002, I met Jasmin, the father of one of the diabetic children. He met with me at the Village Hall and I distributed supplies, money, and gifts to him. Like many others, the families of diabetic children struggled to put food on the table, and many times, it was financially impossible to care for a sick child.

Jasmin provided me with documents from doctors about each child so I knew their stages of diabetes and what they needed. The state supplied insulin to these families, but the families did not have the expensive needles and test strips to monitor blood sugar levels.

On every visit, I tried to spend a day with these children. On one of my trips, a little girl named Vildana gave me a hand-carved box. One of the fathers, an amputee, was a wood carver. Inside the box was a parchment paper with the names of all the children. The cover of the box held the following inscription:

This is just a little gift for your great humanity and friendship.

Over the years, they have given me hand-knit slippers and other gifts to show their appreciation. The Lord says that in giving, we truly receive. The people of this country have given of themselves to me time and time again. I will be forever grateful.

Safe Havens in Sarajevo

Thanks to Brother O'Grady, I always found safe havens in Sarajevo while I was on my missions. One of the places I have been privileged to stay was with the Franciscan Sisters. They live in a modest three-story home on a narrow street. The five nuns always welcome me with open arms. Two are nurses who work at the nearby Kosevo Hospital, two are teachers, and Sister Kata is the cook and house-keeper. Sister Maria, the orthopedic nurse, has been there from the beginning. She is an inspiration to me.

When I stay with the sisters, I live like they do. We rise for 6:30 a.m. mass in the little chapel on the second floor. A priest from the monastery presides. We then enjoy a wonderful Bosnian breakfast of organic vegetables from the sisters' garden, homemade bread, and goat cheese, and plum jam from the Rama region of northern Bosnia, where most of the sisters are from.

On a recent trip, the sisters taught me how to make homemade walnut brandy! They also expressed their sadness that the country is still in crisis. Marriages have dissolved and the young Catholic population has little involvement with the church. Nevertheless, the Franciscan sisters carry on with and faith in the Lord. They are family.

Chapter 6
The Roots of Home Sprout a Forest

None of my efforts to help the people of Bosnia would have been possible had it not been for friends, relatives, co-workers, churches, and total strangers who have contributed supplies for me to bring to the refugees and people in war-torn Bosnia. I cannot speak of my missions without mentioning the loving generosity of people who have contributed to my efforts.

It is one of the most beautiful compensations of this life that no one can sincerely try to help another without helping himself.
—Ralph Waldo Emerson

One of the many compensations I have received are countless lasting and true friendships of people who have worked in the background to make my trips possible. Like a ripple of water, word got out about my work and more and more people contacted me. In a very short time, I became a one-woman relief organization. Never, at age 57, did I think I would be calculating cargo weights and going into war zones.

When national journalists began to chronicle the atrocities in Bosnia and my efforts were written about locally in Milwaukee, people in the United States began to offer help, including my friends and family. Offers of donations and funds came from everywhere. But it did not come until the ravages of war had taken a huge toll on hundreds of thousands of innocent people.

Many wanted to help my efforts because they knew it would go directly to those in most need. Coverage and interviews by newspapers and local TV stations spread the word as I showed photos and talked of the horrors of war.

A Englishman who worked as a security guard at a local hospital donated teddy bears. He told me that all children should have a teddy bear to hug. Through the years, he has donated thousands of cuddly little bears of all sizes. His reward? Photos of smiling children holding his gifts.

Children receive teddy bears in Medjugorje

A grandmother in a small Wisconsin town was a quilt maker. She started sewing colorful crib quilts for me. Others knit baby blankets, puppet mittens, and warm caps. One of the mitten knitters hid religious tracts inside the mittens, which I had to remove before distributing. (I was not there to evangelize.)

Donations included dental and medical equipment, school supplies, and dialysis machines. I brought yarn and knitting needles after I saw two Bosnian grandmothers knitting with their fingers. During the war, many sheep had been slaughtered for food, and yarn was scarce.

Members of my family stepped in when they could. A niece in Detroit started a doll drive. She collected funds to purchase 4,000 small dolls and delivered them to me in her van.

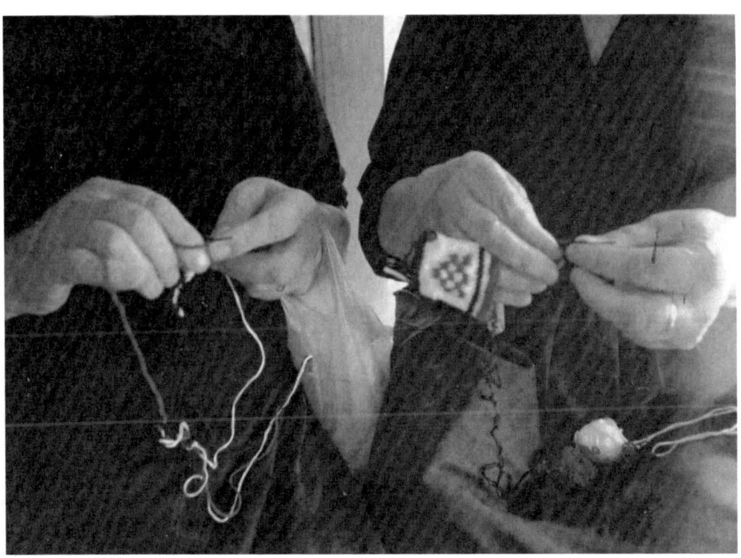

Bosnian grandmothers knitting with their fingers

A cousin had a sock drive in Illinois. Hundreds of socks were donated. A niece started a shoe drive, which spread from Wisconsin to Illinois. Boxes of shoes were collected. While sifting through the stacks of used shoes and discarding those that were too worn, she received a knock on her door late one night. Perfect strangers who had heard of her drive delivered nearly 100 pairs of brand-new shoes. So much charity was out there, so many wonderful people who were willing to help.

When donations started coming in, my first order of business was packaging them to make the 5,000-mile trip across the ocean. Lufthansa Airlines became a great partner and helped with any questions. Everything needed to be shipped at least one week before I was to travel because it took that long for the supplies to arrive.

A group of friends from my community, known as "The Muffins," became a huge support to me during this time. I got to know one member of the group through church before my son Daniel died. She had experienced sorrow in her life and we developed a deep bond. Another woman had been my daughter's friend. She comforted me many times after Danny's death. Another friend I met through church had lost a son years before. So many people close by who had experienced tragedies, but got through so much of it because of their strong faith.

Many friendships are forged as the result of tragic events. Almost every one of us had experienced loss. But every one of us was at peace because we knew we could count on each other and our faith. These women gave me companionship and comfort, and became my foot soldiers to help me carry out my missions!

We started meeting as a group in 1989, gathering at a small cafe every Saturday after mass to enjoy coffee and baked goods. One of the women's daughters referred to us as the "Muffin group." We have kept the name ever since.

When I started to make my solo trips, my Muffin friends asked if they could help. They became experts in packing and sorting my shipments. They came to my house for several days in a row to prepare for my trips, helping to pack and sort and tape the boxes. Getting ready for my trips was more work than I realized, and I could have never done it without them!

One trip, we had 150 boxes. When I weighed them at the airport, they collectively came to close to one ton. One of the Muffins was eager to drive me to the airport for my trips. Another gave me a *Prayer for Soldiers* book when there was still conflict in Bosnia. My Muffins told me much later that they felt as if they were sending me off to war—which of course, they were!

The Muffins were always very relieved when I came home. Many times, they had welcome signs to greet me. When I returned from my trips, I would have them over for breakfast the following Sunday after church, tell them my stories, and show them my pictures.

Sometimes our light goes out but is blown
into flame by another human being.
—Albert Schweitzer

I often think of the family and friends who comforted me and gave emotional support after Danny's death. They were instrumental in helping me for years to come with my missions to Bosnia. Donors of monetary gifts and gifts in-kind had seen articles in local and national publications during the war years. Many of these generous people I have yet to meet. Supplies and checks are still sent to me. The owner of a tavern in Pennsylvania has sent me money for more than twenty years. He is a dear friend though we have never met.

Although I made a decent living as a registered nurse, my trips were slowly beginning to cost more. Donations grew and shipping costs escalated as well. Preparing for a spring trip in 1992, I collected more than 70 boxes of medical supplies, the most I had ever pulled together. I had

Jeanne McCue's grandchildren, Katy, 7, Anne Marie, 4, and Andy, 8, helping her pack for a mission.

no idea what shipping would cost, but felt the Lord would provide. I loaded the supplies into two vans and with a friend, drove them to Chicago's O'Hare International Airport. At the Lufthansa Airlines cargo area, my boxes onto a scale. The cost to ship the supplies was $825. I used my personal credit card and wondered how I would find the money to pay the fee. At the same time, I had a sense of peace and felt it would all work out.

When I returned from the trip, a person from the Human Concerns Committee at my parish contacted me. The next week, I was presented with a check for $850—almost the exact amount I needed to pay for the shipping! From then on, I never worried about resources.

A few years later, when Bill Janz of the *Milwaukee Sentinel* accompanied me to Bosnia, I told him it would be nice to make up a pack for each refugee with all of the necessities in one simple package. Bill wrote about my needs, and suddenly scout groups, churches, schools, and everyday people put together packs for me.

Children's packs had vitamins, toys, toothpaste, a toothbrush, and a box of crayons. The packs were a hit. When I delivered them to eager children, they took them and clutched them to their hearts.

Adult packs had toiletries like soaps, shampoo, vitamins and disposable shavers for men.

When a doctor from Children's Hospital of Wisconsin found out about my trips, he, his wife, and six children created an assembly line in their home to make new mommy and baby packs. They included starter diapers,

Preparing to accompany the many packages of humanitarian aid materials are co-author Peg Masterson Edquist and her husband, Jerry, at O'hare International Airport in Chicago (1992)

nursing gown, toiletries, and vitamins. In winter, we would put in mittens and caps for the children.

Coordinating the assembly of the packs was necessary because I wanted the contents to be uniform. I spent time before and after work, as well as weekends, getting the donations, listing inventory, and packing.

Since the tragic attacks of 9/11, airlines have been very strict about cargo. Every item in the boxes had to be accounted for. One well-intended soul donated 15 boxes, filled with T-shirts and medical supplies. When I realized he had not itemized the supplies, all of the boxes needed to be unpacked and repacked.

The trips were just part of my missions. Getting donations became an ongoing activity. Even though at times I was exhausted with planning and preparation, it was exhilarating to know we were making a difference.

Another wonderful compensation was giving these supplies directly to those who needed them the most. Many times, I took pictures of the children and adults who were overjoyed with my gifts. Every photo shows their gratitude. It has been a joy to show the donors and others what a difference they can make.

Back at home, graphic news of the Balkan war appeared in daily newspapers and on TV. Requests for me to speak and offers to help came from churches, schools, and scout groups. The Allentown 4-H Club in a small Wisconsin farm

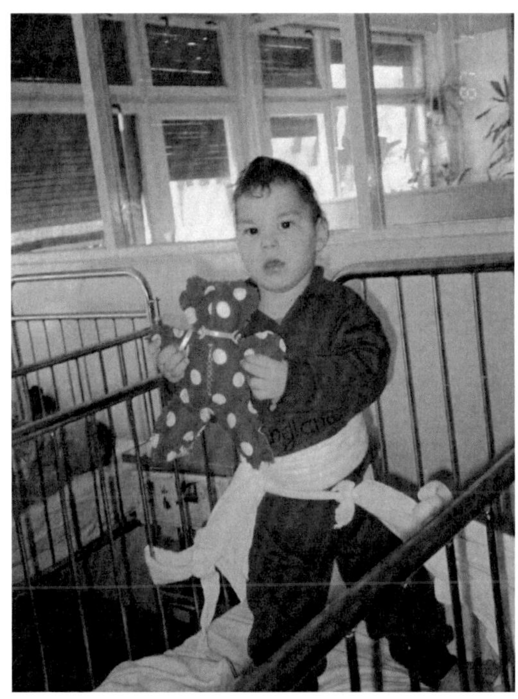

A child with a donated bear in the pediatric section of a hospital in Mostar

community asked to see my slides and hear of my humanitarian travels.

When I arrived, to my delight, the club donated hundreds of seed packets. Refugees in Sarajevo used the seeds to grow cabbage and other vegetables on any green space they could find. Apartment dwellers planted them in window boxes.

In-kind kind donations came from everywhere. They came by mail or were left at my door. Scout groups assembled refugee packs filled with hygiene items. A Harley rider donated money for Bibles. Donations of hearing aids, talking watches for the blind, wooden legs, and vestments for the Croatian priests arrived. A fifth grader asked her friends to bring gifts for Bosnian children to her birthday party. The kindness, caring and generosity was energizing.

Women in downtown Sarajevo tend to a makeshift garden to grow food during the war

A few years after I began to travel to Bosnia, I started a newsletter for those who donated to my efforts. I inserted photos and memories of my most recent trips and listed the needs for my upcoming trips. This amazing journey has made me as much of a communicator as I have ever been since embarking on my missions.

I am also indebted to all those who were with me on my journeys. Numerous trips were made alone during the early years of the conflict. Later, amazing friends and family members accompanied me. It gave them great insight into the work we were accomplishing and the challenges that we faced.

Along my entire journey, friends and family have been amazed that I have continued my personal mission to help the people of Bosnia. Although it has been more than twenty years, I feel no need to slow down as long as I'm healthy and active. This kind of humanitarian work is addictive. When I return from these trips, I experience a natural high for days because I feel I have made a difference in people's lives. When the adrenaline returns to normal levels, I begin to think about my next trip!

It's no use saying,
"We are doing our best."
You have got to succeed
in doing what is necessary.
—Winston Churchill

Chapter 7
The Narrow Road

It is often hard to take the road less traveled, the one that presents challenges along the way and is filled with unknowns. When we are at a loss, we usually end up at a place we never thought we would be. For me, the road less traveled was the path to take. I never imagined I would spend so much of my adult life on a singular mission.

But after Daniel died and I lost my way in grief, I found that the difficult road was best for me. Throughout this journey, my faith has been the one constant. It has carried me when I could not imagine life without my son. It helped me make the first step in helping others. It has delivered so much to me, not only in spiritual comfort, but tangible signs, from surprise donations to monetary assistance when I needed it the most.

Even in the darkest days of the war, when I was surrounded by active gunfire or mortar shelling, God was with me and I wore Him like a plate of armor. I never had fear or doubt in all these years that He would deliver me safely to the people of Bosnia and safely back to my home.

The trip in 1995, when I rode in the United Nations tank rumbling toward Sarajevo, will stay with me forever. I was 59 years old, alone, living out a spiritual calling that had turned my life upside down, but I was never more energized and peaceful at the same time. At that moment, so far away from home in such a dangerous place, I knew it was the right place for me to be.

Throughout the past 20-plus years, the focus of my aid changed with the needs of the people. At first, life-saving supplies were needed by hospitals and collective centers. After the Dayton Peace Accord, requests came for home health supplies for hospices, schools and dental supplies for orphanages and Roma children, funds for the elderly poor's soup kitchens, and to purchase goats to enable displaced families to return to their village farms.

On every mission and under so many varied conditions, my faith called me to Bosnia. When I answered God's call to serve, the messages of the Gospel unfolded before me. In different cities and towns and in so many circumstances, I felt God at my side, working with me and providing the resources I needed. The donations of supplies and funds multiplied like loaves and fishes. The support of generous family members and friends turned my "mourning into dancing" (Psalm 30).

I began to see the post-war poverty phase in Bosnia and received requests to cover the home health needs of Njega, the first home hospice, from the Irish Sisters of the Cross and Passion. I met the diabetic children of Zavidovici and brought supplies and funds to monitor and control their disease. After I saw senior citizens searching dumpsters for food after dusk, I helped fund The Bread of St. Anthony soup kitchens in Sarajevo. And so the work continues.

A Legacy Moves Forward

My first trip to Bosnia in 1992 set the stage for a lifetime of joy, which I found over and over again was when I placed myself in the service of others.

My hope is that my lasting legacy will be to share the work I have done with others and that it will inspire them to do the same. Together we can continue to fill the places we live and visit with joy every day.

As I have seen my life trickle down to those I touched in Bosnia, I have also seen it seep into my family.

My grandchildren have grown up watching the effort, dedication, and raw courage that always laid the foundation for my missions. As little children, they helped sort donations and pack supplies in my rec room. They worried at night, prayed at the church on Sundays while I was gone, were eager to see photos of refugee children, and hear my stories of the war when I returned home. As their lives continue to unfold, they have experienced their own joy in the service of others. My grandchildren inspire me as they serve the poor and sick here in the US and around the world.

My granddaughter, Katy Grennier, traveled with me to Bosnia while she was in college. She had begged to go for years. When Katy was a young girl, she made it a priority to volunteer in soup kitchens and youth programs. Her undergraduate studies in social work and her strong desire to help others led her to jobs around the US to advocate for underprivileged youth.

Katy's service path eventually led her to the Clinton School of Public Service in Little Rock, Arkansas, where she earned a Master's degree in Public Service. Katy has spent the last several years in countries in Africa and Asia creating educational programs that allow youth to have an advocate—a voice when it matters most.

My grandson, Andrew Grennier, has dedicated his life to the service of others by becoming a nurse. After coming home from the war in Afghanistan, he decided he had seen enough pain and was determined to commit the rest of his life to helping the sick. He worked as a nurse at the Milwaukee Veterans Administration Hospital and brought joy to the patients with his humor and his big heart.

Another grandson, Braden, works as an advocate for homeless youth. Although he is young, he has mature empathy and sincerely cares for others. I am always heartened when the younger generation shows initiative to care about others less fortunate.

Bosnia Today

One of the main reasons I have continued my missions is because the people in Bosnia still suffer. The government is ruled by three factions, representing the Muslims, Croats, and Serbs. While the hope was to rule together in harmony, divisiveness has created a country with rulers who cannot find consensus.

Employment in 2014 in Bosnia hovered around 44 percent, affecting almost every household. I still see the agony on people's faces during my most recent visits. It may not be the pain of direct warfare, but rather that of poverty, division, and discord.

William Norris, in a 2013 article, for the Borgen Project of Seattle, $100 billion worth of damage was inflicted on the country during the war. Nearly half the Bosnia-Herzegovina population fled the country following the conflict. The impact has been significant, making it one of the poorest countries in Europe.

In an article in *USA Today* published in February, 2014, reporters wrote that citizens are pressing for change, saying the unrest reflects mounting frustrations at a dysfunctional political system and a failing economy that is a product of a flawed peace agreement signed nearly 20 years ago.

My young friend and interpreter, Ana-Marija, who was a teenager during the war, told me that the memories of war are locked inside little boxes in their brains and sometimes come out. More than 20 years later, thousands of second-generation teenage victims of the Balkan War struggle with violence and substance abuse, in large part because their parents were never treated for war trauma. Domestic violence has greatly increased in the country. Thousands of veterans have PTSD and suffer from hunger due to lack of pensions. More than 4,000 suicides have occurred since the end of the war.

The destruction from the war in Bosnia-Herzegovina remains ever-present in the country. Poverty has ruled most of the population since the war ended. Buildings still stand with gashes from the heavy mortar fire. Others are abandoned with few resources to either rebuild or tear down.

One article in *USA Today* reported that the majority of poverty resides in rural areas, where the failures of the market economy have become evident. Farmers are most heavily impacted, and nearly 90 percent of their livestock were killed in the struggle. More than half of their assets were lost.

The people who remain in Bosnia are beginning to be heard. Protests have filled the streets of Sarajevo with citizens demanding better wages, better pensions, and more opportunities to improve their way of lives.

In a BBC report in the spring 2014, reporter Guy Delany covered widespread protests across the entire country that caused damage to government buildings in several cities.

> *....Anyone thinking Bosnia's protests were strictly a matter of disenchanted youth might have changed their mind after a Sunday in Sarajevo.... Tomislav Bajkusa, 81, pulled out an ID card which showed that he had been a concentration camp prisoner during the Balkan conflict of the 1990s. Then he produced his monthly pension statement. It amounted to 380 convertible marks a month, about $265, to look after three people, including his adult son, who Mr. Bajkusa said, had not been able to find a job since 1992.*
>
> *I want to be proud of my country again—this country as it is now is not functional," he said. "I would love to see the youth gathered here today to get jobs and be happy. Nobody's happy anymore—nobody smiles, I don't smile. Even the soil we are standing on is crying.*

The Work Continues

Much of my work today consists of running a goat program, which I established several years ago, as well as bringing much-needed donations to several charitable organizations.

To a hungry refugee family in Bosnia, the gift of a goat is an important step toward becoming self-reliant for food and income. It gives them the opportunity to return to their village farms and provide for themselves. Displaced families returning to their farms are in need of livestock.

A goat is a poor man's cow. Goats thrive in poor conditions and can give as much as four quarts of milk a day. A family with a goat has milk to drink, and can make butter and cheese to sell.

I first purchased a goat in 1993, when a villager in Medjugorje told me of an older couple who was caring for their two young grandchildren whose parents had been killed in Sarajevo. They lived on a farm a few miles from Mostar and needed a goat to provide milk. I bought a goat for $150 and hired a driver in a small compact car. We put the goat in the back seat and surprised the happy grandparents with our gift. I also gave them seeds from the Allenton, Wisconsin, 4-H group.

In 2003, Ljubica Jelic, a wonderful Croatian woman in Milwaukee, asked me to give a donation of $100 to a Croatian priest in Sarajevo. She had never met him, but he had the same surname as she did. When I arrived on my mission, I contacted Father Anton Jelic of Catholic Croatian Charities. We had a wonderful exchange and on a subsequent trip, he gave me goat cheese to bring home. He had purchased a goat with Ljubica's donation. That was the start of the goat program. Through the years, Father Jelic has helped to identify which families are in the most need. Since it began, our program has provided funds to purchase more than 2,500 goats.

When I'm not brokering a goat donation, most of my work is visiting several organizations that continue to serve the poor and the disenfranchised. Those include Egipat Children's Home, Njega Hospice, Roma children, the diabetic children of Zavidovici, and The Bread of St. Anthony. Each time I travel to Bosnia, the gratitude of the people is overwhelming. The ability to the human spirit to endure so much suffering and yet offer thanks for what is given is humbling.

(L to R): A proud goat farmer, Jeanne McCue, and Father Jelic in Travnik, Bosnia

While working in the country during the most dangerous of times, I wanted to be an instrument of peace. Cardinal Puljic wrote about peace in 1992; his words continue to hold relevance today:

> *So many lives have been cruelly ended. Thousands of wounded will for the rest of their days carry their wounds. So many children will never rid themselves of the trauma of war. So many of our mothers and sisters have been warped and humiliated by rape. All the spiritual wounds and corroded hearts lie among people like a dark shadow allowing hate to seep in. The inversion of the human heart is essential in time of war. If we cannot care for men's hearts and free them from the poison of hate, there will be no better tomorrows.*
>
> (Excerpt from "Suffering with Hope")

Meaningful Coincidences

Throughout all of my journeys, God's hand has been at my side protecting, encouraging, and giving me courage. I am constantly reminded of Him when I experience "meaningful coincidences" (little miracles), which are not coincidences at all, but God giving us connections, signs and direction.

We live in a world in which nothing happens by chance. Perhaps this is divine providence. Miracles happen every day if only we recognize them for what they are. They all seem to have the "fingerprints of God."

Sometimes when I feel troubled, I open a scripture. My son Daniel had donated a children's water fountain near our neighborhood school several years before his death. He had been a crossing guard at the corner when he was younger. Six months after his death, I attended an all-night prayer vigil in the church across the street from the fountain. I had asked God to someday give me a sign that Daniel was in Heaven. Moments later, I opened my Bible to this passage:

Whoever gives only a cup of water to one of these little ones – he will surely not lose his reward.
—Matthew 10:42

God is so good.

Waiting at the Split Airport in Croatia to return to the States, I had a chance meeting with an Irish brother, Thomas O'Grady. He might never have stopped to talk to me if he had not seen a little shamrock I had on one of my bags.

In the fall of 2004, I was in Chicago's O'Hare Airport awaiting a flight to Munich and Sarajevo. A toddler held by her father had lost her shoe, which I had found under a bench. The father turned out to be a concert pianist from Minnesota, who was flying to give a benefit concert for an organization in Sarajevo run by his brother.

His brother, who lived in Sarajevo, met him there and invited me to the concert at the old music hall downtown. After the concert, they inquired about my missions. When the brother returned to Minnesota, they collected and sent me funds for my mission.

On a November flight to Sarajevo in 1995, I missed a connecting flight in Frankfurt to Sarajevo via Zagreb. After waiting hours for the last flight of the day, I was exhausted. I climbed the airport steps to a chapel and found an inspirational leaflet from the *Word of Life* publication sitting on a table. Everything that was written in that issue was about perseverance. The top of the leaflet read,

Your perseverance will win you your lives.
—Luke 21:19

Throughout the church's history, Christians have reached fulfillment of their goals from a particular strength or virtue. Mine is perseverance. This word, with Greek origins, has other meanings, including patience, steadfastness, trust, and endurance in the face of all difficulties. Throughout my life, I have always been blessed with perseverance in challenging situations. In Romans 15:5, St. Paul refers to "... the God of steadfastness and encouragement."

During my nursing career, I have heard physicians explain the benefits and risks about a procedure/treatment to their patients. Looking back, my missions had risks, but the benefits far outweighed those risks. I also learned that when we help other's carry their burdens of poverty, sickness and grief, our own burdens become lighter.

My Bosnian Friends Comfort Those Who Comfort

When tragedy struck New York City on September 11, 2001, the images of the World Trade Center in ruins reminded me of my visits to Sarajevo during the war. At the time, my friends who lived through such horror shared our sorrow. The people I comforted for so many years were now lending their support and comfort. They wrote:

Dear Jeanne,
We were all very shocked and saddened by the dreadful attacks in New York and Washington yesterday and we want you to know that we are thinking of you and all the people who have been hurt or killed and their families.

—The NJEGA Hospice Staff

Dear Jeanne,
My heart goes out to the American people in solidarity this day. No words can describe the terrible situation which occurred last Tuesday September 11th. May God Bless America in its hour of suffering. God bless and love you,

—Brother Thomas O'Grady

Dear Jeanne,
This is beyond words. Every attempt to describe the horror, shock and outrage is failure compared to the extent and depth of Tuesday's tragedy. Our hearts, minds and prayers are with you and your country.

—Psychosocial Trauma Recovery Department, CRS Sarajevo

Dear Lady Jeanne,
As soon as I heard those monstrosities that happened in your country I got in touch with Lady Irene (traveling companion). I feared something had happened to you and her. I am relieved to know that you are OK. I wish you and the US all the best. God bless,

—Zlatko (our driver)

Lessons of Lost Luggage

So many times in my missions, I faced obstacles that turned into positive messages that renewed my faith in my work.

In January 1994, I traveled to Bosnia for the fifth time. I was traveling alone and due to storms in the United States, my outbound flight was canceled. When I finally got on a plane, it flew to Italy and then Croatia. When I arrived in Italy, my luggage was not there. I had a carry-on with a portable EKG machine. My personal items, warm boots and mittens were in my checked luggage. My flight to Croatia was re-routed due to high winds over the Adriatic and the Croatian mountains. We landed in Zagreb and flew to Croatia the next morning.

Gojko was waiting for me when I arrived, but my luggage did not make it. We drove through the snow to Medjugorje. It was very cold. Because I had nothing to keep me warm but my travel clothes, I slept in them for two weeks during the entire trip.

The inconvenience reminded me that the refugees do not have any personal items, no warm clothes, and not even their own beds to lie in. They had fled their homes without any belongings and could never return. It was a blessing to understand their circumstances and double my efforts to help them. I could go back home to the comfort of my life. For them, this was their life.

My supplies had also been delayed. For two days, I did not have any medical supplies to hand out. For the first time in my life, until the cargo arrived days later, I had nothing to give, beyond my smile and my caring.

Obstacles of Fear

My journeys to Bosnia have been journeys of faith. Faith has its own logic, which defies common sense. Each time I traveled to the war-torn country, I became more convinced of God's love and protection and the power of prayer. Like a child thrown into mid-air, who falls back into the safety of its parent's loving arms, I knew God would catch me no matter what.

The paths I followed that allowed me to witness hardship and suffering brought me closer to God. The more suffering I witnessed, the more I felt the power of God's love propelling me to return with assistance again and again. Although my family was concerned about my well-being and safety, I knew that wherever I went, He was with me.

In the hidden corners of a country devastated by war, I found the cold and dimly lit rooms of refugee centers, unheated school rooms, dark and damp apartments, and suffering from the very young to the very old. But I also found happy school children in winter coats grateful for my supplies, and the elderly, who would give me their last piece of bread as a token of their gratitude. The people of Bosnia exuded generosity in the midst of suffering; how could I not be generous with all the tools and resources God had given me?

Hope

Of all the forces that make for a better world,
none is so powerful as Hope.
With hope one can think, one can work
and one can dream.
If you have hope, you have everything.
—Author unknown

Throughout more than two decades of bringing humanitarian aid to Bosnian refugees, I always sensed their hope—hope they would return to their village and their homes, reunite with loved ones and neighbors, and see better tomorrows for their children. C.S. Lewis wrote of joy:

> *Joy can be distinguished from happiness and pleasure. Joy has one characteristic in common with them. The fact that anyone who has experienced Joy will want it again and again. Anyone who has tasted it would not exchange it for all the pleasures of the world.*

During the worst part of the conflict, I saw the smiles on the faces of children in their dismal refugee camps. I often wondered how people bore the destruction of their homes and separation from loved ones.

Hope is an action word for me. Life leaps forward to new and unknown places. Hope moves us to respond to God's invitation. We often commit ourselves to serve, not knowing where the path may lead. My path led me to Bosnia, where I found peace and experienced the joy of giving.

peace
is deciding to
live
together
again.

Resources & References

Bell, Martin. BBC World News report, January 1994

Delany, Guy. BBC World News report, 2014

Harris, Paul. *Cry Bosnia*, Northhampton, MA: Interlink Publishing Group, 1995

Janz, William. Series on Jeanne McCue's missions to Bosnia, *Milwaukee Sentinel*, November 1993

Jolie, Angelina. *The Land of Blood and Honey*, GK Films United States December 2011

Kapic, Suada. *Sarajevo Survival Guide*. FAMA International Media company, 1992-1995

Nelson, Bill. "Children in War," *Milwaukee Journal*, March 27, 1994

Neuffer, Elizabeth. *The Key to my Neighbors House: Seeking Justice in Bosnia and Rwanda*. New York: Picador, 2001

Norris, William. *Post-war struggles: Poverty in Bosnia-Herzegovina*. The Borgen Project, Seattle, Washington. July 2013

Rhode, David. "Grave Confirms Bosnia Massacre." *Christian Science Monitor*, November 16, 1995

Serenelli, Luighi, Jahnic, DIno. "Citizens Pressing for Change in Bosnia," *USA Today*, February 27, 2014

Vesilind, Priit J. "In Focus: Bosnia," *National Geographic* 189 issue No. 3 March 1996

Vinko, Cardinal Puljic. *Suffering with Hope: Appeals, Addresses, Interviews*. Zagreb, Napredak, 1995

Co-authors Jeanne McCue and Peg Masterson Edquist
on the historic bridge where Austrian Archduke Franz Ferdinand
was assassinated on June 14, 1914, to start World War I.

About the Authors

Jeanne McCue is a retired registered nurse who worked a total of 55 years at St. Mary's Hospital, Milwaukee County General Hospital and Froedtert Hospital, all in the Milwaukee area. After she began her mission trips in 1994, she founded Bosnia Relief Charitable Trust www.bosniarelief.org/.

Since her mission work began, Jeanne has won numerous awards and recognitions. They include a nomination for Wisconsin Nurse of the Year in 1992, Woman of Distinction Award by Cardinal Stritch University in Milwaukee, in 1993. The Extra Mile Award from Froedtert Hospital in 2000, the Shaklee Community Caretaker Award by Shaklee National Nutrition Corporation in San Francisco, in 2001, the Gold Leaf Award from Friendship Village in Milwaukee in 2003, the Milwaukee Academy of Medicine Award by the Medical College of Wisconsin in 2003. In 2005, Jeanne received the Health Care Hero award from Froedtert Hospital, Milwaukee, and was named to the Milwaukee County Senior Hall of Fame. In 1996, Jeanne was selected as an official torch bearer for the Summer Olympics in Atlanta, Georgia, that year.

Peg Masterson Edquist is an award-winning journalist and freelance writer. She received her undergraduate degree in Mass Communication from the University of Wisconsin—Milwaukee in 1981. She worked as an editor of an electronic news service for Journal Communications in Milwaukee, as a morning news anchor at a Milwaukee area radio station, and as a reporter at the *Milwaukee Sentinel*, where she won an Inland Daily Press Association award for local news coverage.

Peg was a freelance magazine writer for *The Writer*, *Advertising Age*, and *Photo District News*. She was a contributing writer and columnist for the *Business Journal of Greater Milwaukee* for 20 years.

Peg is co-author of *Love, Power, & Money: Family Business Between Generations*, with Dean Fowler.

In 2011, she traveled with her aunt, Jeanne McCue, to Sarajevo to conduct research for this book and assisted in the creation of the website for the Bosnia Relief Charitable Trust, www.bosniarelief.org.